Be your own best life coach

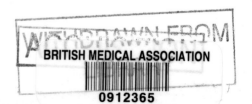

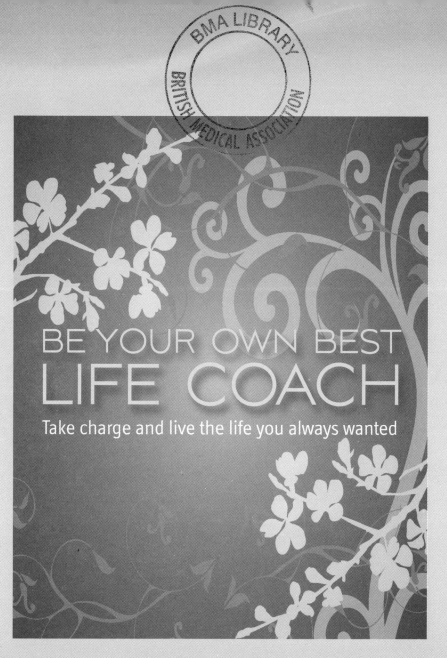

BE YOUR OWN BEST
LIFE COACH

Take charge and live the life you always wanted

Jackee Holder

brilliantideas

Careful now

Athough the contents of this book were checked at the time of going to press, the Internet is constantly being updated. This means the publisher and author cannot guarantee the contents of any of the websites mentioned.

First published in 2009 by
Infinite Ideas Limited
36 St Giles
Oxford, OX1 3LD
United Kingdom
www.infideas.com

A CIP catalogue record for this book is available from the British Library

ISBN 978-1-905940-65-3

Brand and product names are trademarks or registered trademarks of their respective owners.

Designed and typeset by Baseline Arts Ltd, Oxford
Printed in India

Brilliant ideas

Brilliant features

Each chapter of this book is designed to provide you with an inspirational idea that you can read quickly and put into practice straight away.

Throughout you'll find three features that will help you get right to the heart of the idea:

- *Here's an idea for you* Take it on board and give it a go – right here, right now. Get an idea of how well you're doing so far.

- *Defining idea* Words of wisdom from masters and mistresses of the art, plus some interesting hangers-on.

- *How did it go?* If at first you do succeed, try to hide your amazement. If, on the other hand, you don't, then this is where you'll find a Q and A that highlights common problems and how to get over them.

Introduction

Life coaches are a great resource. Well, I would say that, wouldn't I, since I am a coach and it's a job that I love. But I also believe with a passion that you don't need to pay a coach (because some of us do charge quite a hefty fee) to help you transform your life.

For years I've invested time and money in therapy, courses, several coaches, workshops and training; don't get me wrong – they were all good and I met some great people along the way. But when the courses were over and I'd come down off my high, I was still left with the task of putting what I had learnt into practice. At the end of the day, no matter how brilliant someone is and no matter how great the information they have to share with you, it won't make the blindest bit of difference unless you act on it – and that's where the real work begins.

That's why I always tell my clients my job is to coach myself out of a job. I hold this expectation for every single one of the great people I get to work with, people from all walks of life, some facing a major crisis, others wanting to improve and build on their successes. Whoever they are, I see in each person a glorious potential to becoming their own best life coach. That's why I wrote this book, so you could have that information in one place. Coaching is one of the most generous professions I know of when it comes to sharing information. Coaching is also a way of life. So what better than to share some of what I have learnt over the years with you in a book that is guaranteed to help you transform your life? I know this because the exercises I have included have worked for me as well as hundreds of coaching clients and workshop participants that I have helped and supported over the years. Personally these ideas have helped me take control of my time management. They have seen me create time and space in my busy life for regular creativity and self-care. And more than anything the ideas have helped me feel better and clearer about my life, fuelling me with the confidence to make small changes that keep on reaping bigger and better results.

This wasn't always the case. A turning point happened for me about six years ago. I found myself at a crossroads. Even though on the outside it looked like my life was going very well, inside I was really struggling. I kept thinking there must be more than this. And I kept wishing that the right coach or person would come along who would miraculously have the right formula to help me change my life. That person showed up in the form of one of the UK's top life coaches. I got in contact, sure that this time I had found the coach who would push the magic button and, hey presto, my life would change. I signed up and enthusiastically agreed to hand over £175 for my first two-hour coaching session, the most I had ever forked out for a life coach.

Part of the agreement on signing up for the session was to complete a form where I would provide a bit of background and highlight my goals and challenges. In the run-up to my session I got really busy, then my computer wasn't working and before I knew it I was two days away from meeting my new coach and my form was still incomplete. In my haste to get on top of things and with my email playing up I thought, no problem, I'll just fax it. I contacted the office. Turned out they didn't have a fax. Eventually that evening the coach called me. After a ten-minute conversation she calmly announced that she didn't think I was ready to be coached.

I've got to give it to her: she calmly walked away from her £175 fee. This was a huge wake-up call. I made the decision then and there that if I wanted to change my life I had to change and I couldn't rely on other people to have the magic formulae to change it for me.

Since my sacking six years ago my life has gone from strength to strength. While I'm not proud of that moment when I got sacked as a client, I'm proud of the learning I took from it. I went on to successfully train as a coach, to build a healthy coaching practice and to work on a range of creative and inspiring learning programmes that have all been part of my dream life and career. Of course there have been challenges along the way but with my newfound confidence these are handled. Not bad for a woman who as a child experienced sexual abuse, as a teenager physical assault from her then boyfriend and who has battled with low self-esteem, confidence and many of life's addictions. If I can do it, so can you.

You'll find that the ideas I share with you are the same tools coaches use when coaching. Consider this your own personal training programme in becoming your own best life coach. It will help tremendously if you keep a notebook and pen close by (I always have one with me wherever I go). Your notebook will come in handy for jotting down observations and thoughts that come from any of the ideas you try out as well as making connections. Like most changes, some may happen instantly and others may take time. That's why it's a good idea to make a daily commitment. What happened yesterday is history. Your power and ability to transform your life lies in the changes and decisions you make today. I hope that these 52 ideas will support you in creating and living your best life. Enjoy the journey and, above all, don't forget that you more than any other person have the power and potential within to become your own best life coach.

Jackee

Wheel
of Life Tree

8

7

1

6

2

5

3

4

KEY:

Fulfilled

Incomplete

1. _____

2. _____

3. _____

4. _____

5. _____

6. _____

7. _____

8. _____

© Jackee Holder

1. Tools of the trade

The moment you stop what you're doing and start reviewing your life is the time you begin a process of change.

The Wheel of Life Tree is the perfect tool to find out how you're doing.

Before you get started here's something I want you to do: invest in a packet of colouring pencils or box of crayons. Parents of toddlers or young children hopefully won't have to look far. For everyone else a quick trip to Woolies (that's Woolworths for short), your local pound shop or W.H. Smith's will do the trick. I know you haven't done colouring in since you were a kid but, hey, it's good to bring a bit of play into serious matters.

You'll need a copy of a blank Wheel of Life Tree: feel free to photocopy the one in this book or download a copy from www.jackeeholder.com. Begin by deciding which areas of your life each of the eight wheels represents. This is not just about choosing areas that are all sorted but also about the areas you'd like to make better. Here are some ideas for areas you might include.

- Career and Life Purpose
- Finances and Money
- Home and Environment
- Health and Well-being
- Leisure and Social Time
- Relationships and Friendships

Here's an idea for you...

Pick an area of your life you'd like to improve and describe what it would look like, feel like, sound or smell like if it was operating at its best. Now assess that area by giving yourself a score on a scale of 0 to 10, with 10 representing this area working at its best and 0 representing it at its worst. Focus on the gap between where you are and where you want to be and brainstorm a list of actions that will move you closer towards a 10. Take one action in the next 24 hours.

- Spirituality and Religion
- Creativity and Inspiration
- Travel and Adventure
- Personal Style and Fashion

These are just suggestions. You'll know better than anyone what areas to include on your list. Use the eight lines at the bottom of the tree to label each of the wheels so you know what areas of your life they relate to.

Now's your chance to consider just how well each area is actually working. Don't worry, this is not about emerging with a glowing assessment. Very few of us make it to that place of perfect balance. In fact, the more honest you are, the better. I remember being on a course with other coaches and feeling under pressure to present a Wheel of Life that looked really balanced (talk about competition among your peers).

Each of the rings in each life wheel represents a sliding scale running from 1, which is the centre ring, to 5, which is the final ring at the edge of each wheel. If you rate an area of your life as a 1, it means that overall you're not happy with that area and recognise that there's room for lots of improvement. So shade in one ring only. Colouring or shading in three rings from the centre reflects the parts of this area that are working well but you know with a bit more input it could be even better. Colouring in all five rings means you feel fulfilled and satisfied with this area of your life (in which case give yourself a pat on the back).

By the way, have you noticed how relaxing colouring is and how it actually slows you down? As you colour or shade in each life wheel, be honest. Remember this is for your eyes only. Your tree will quickly identify the areas not getting as much attention as you'd like and the areas that are working just fine. Right now you might want to ask yourself: 'What actions can I take to regain balance?'

Is your tree full of colour or lacking in a particular colour? Would you consider this a tree in the winter of its life? A tree in its autumn? Or a tree in full bloom? What does each wheel tell you about the overall health of that area of your life right now? Write a list of actions for each wheel that will help you improve the quality of each area. It's a good idea to focus on one area at a time so you don't get overwhelmed. As you make progress don't forget to colour in another ring. You can complete a new Wheel of Life Tree in three or six months' time to see how your tree may have changed.

In the midst of winter, I finally learned that there was in me an invincible summer.

Albert Camus, winner of the Nobel Prize in Literature 1957

How did it go?

Q. There's hardly any colour on my tree and now I'm even more miserable than I was before I completed it. Any thoughts on what I could do to pep myself up?

A. I know it can feel disheartening but at least now you're fully aware and engaged with what isn't working and you're in a great position to do something about it. Concentrate on the action you're going to take over the coming weeks and months. It helps to focus on one area at a time. Small changes done over time add up and often have an impact on other areas, so learn to be patient; it will serve you well.

Q. I don't get it. Are we meant to be focusing on the areas of our lives that we want to improve or do we choose just any area to focus on?

A. It's really up to you. If there are eight areas you want to improve then go for it. However, it may be more rewarding to also include areas that are working well. Positive reinforcement is good. On days when you're not feeling great, just being reminded about what is working well in your life can be extremely motivating. It's not realistic to think you'll have everything sorted out in all areas of your life at the same time. That's an ideal, rarely a reality.

2. Coaching one on one

The aim of this idea is really simple: you'll carve out the time in your busy schedule to meet with yourself, on a regular basis.

The first habit you're asked to cultivate is to set up regular meetings with yourself where you'll get into the habit of engaging in quality time to think and what entrepreneur Michael E. Gerber, author of *The E-myth Revisited*, describes as not just working in your life but working on your life.

Would you normally hesitate about scheduling in times and appointments for just about every other individual in your life? Well, now's the time to do the opposite so, before you even think about talking yourself out of it, how about getting your diary out right now and scheduling in your first coaching session? Work out when in your day would be the best time to meet up with you. Look for a time in the day when you have the most energy and are most unlikely to be distracted. For me that's early morning between 5 and 7 a.m. (I know I'm a bit of an early bird). But maybe around 9 p.m. after the children have gone to bed works better for you. It helps to plan ahead so why not write your next four sessions in your diary now? Once it goes into your diary it gives it greater importance.

Here's an idea for you...

Make a list of all the activities that you do every day from brushing your teeth and taking a shower to travelling to work. Include almost every single activity you can think of including the hours that you sleep. There are 1,440 minutes in a day. Is there an activity or group of activities you could stop doing or ones where the length of time could be reduced? Use the saved time to create space in your week for your regular solo coaching session.

It's a good idea to have your sessions at the same time each week (daily would be great but not essential) so it becomes a habit. The good news is that you'll get to decide how long your sessions will be. But ten minutes as a minimum seems to really work (any less and you might as well stay in bed). That means making a commitment to spend at least ten minutes with yourself.

You may also find that having a trigger in place is a helpful reminder for your coaching sessions. You could set an alarm on your watch or mobile phone, leave yourself a voicemail message or send yourself a text. Or your stimulus for your sessions might be the aroma of a cup of coffee at a certain time each day, which becomes your trigger. Once you've sat down with your steaming cup of coffee (alone) it's also a signal to spend some time thinking about you. So you might anchor this trigger by sitting quietly for ten minutes or spending time writing in your notebook. Decide now on what trigger will provide the cue for your coaching session and how you will anchor it. Don't forget to change your triggers after two or three months when they start being not so effective.

Don't worry, there are no restrictions as to where you hold your solo coaching sessions. Hold them in bed (as long as you're in bed alone), parked up in your car, on a park bench, in a crowded café, on the loo (not sure how hygienic that would be), in the bath or on the top of a double-decker bus.

I know you're thinking, what on earth am I meant to do with myself in my sessions? One of the easiest and simplest things you could do is just allow yourself to sit and be silent. One of your goals will be getting used to hearing your own thoughts and drilling down to your own inner wisdom. You'll only retrieve that wisdom (great ideas will eventually emerge on the tail-end of a whole bunch of crappy ones) once you give yourself regular time and space to think. Try it right now. Don't do anything for the next ten minutes. Just sit quietly and be. When the ten minutes is up, ask yourself this question: 'In that time, what is the one thought that came to me that was useful?' Write it down. The more you cultivate time to think, the more benefits you'll gain.

Most of us would do more for another than we would do for ourselves. Unfortunately we can only do for one another what we can really do for ourselves. Tonya Pinkins, actress

How did it go?

Q. I haven't been able to stick to my one on one coaching sessions. I'd planned to do them in the morning but the mornings just seem to run away with me. Any suggestions?

A. Is your session really the absolutely first thing you do in your day? So in your case that would mean before you even move out of bed or wipe the sleep from your eyes. Instead why not reach over for your notebook or just lie there for ten minutes with your thoughts.

Q. This all seems really simple and straightforward and not aimed at someone like me. How do I go about training as a life coach online?

A. Go online and search for coaching courses and hundreds of different courses will pop up. I'd recommend looking up the International Coach Federation and the Association For Coaching. But at the core of any good, high-quality coaching course will be your relationship with yourself. All the top-end coaches invest heavily in their own personal development. These ideas help you build on your relationship with yourself, which is essential development work not only as a coach but also as a worthy and healthy human being. I suggest trying out the ten minutes of silence for the next seven days and observing the impact.

3. Write it down and make it happen

The notebook, long on the scene well before the first ever computer showed its face, is undergoing something of a revival. The notebook is a great holding place for your ideas, creative thinking and other bits and pieces.

Artists, thinkers and entrepreneurs like Van Gogh, Picasso, Ernest Hemingway, Richard Branson and Paul Smith (I know they're all men) have used notebooks to sketch, paint, make notes, flesh out ideas for their business empires, outline stories and capture original thoughts.

If you're not currently using a notebook maybe now is a good time to give it a try. OK, so you're probably a laptop or BlackBerry junkie, but hear me out. Notebooks provide the ideal space to engage in creative and quality thinking. Start-up costs are low, it doesn't need booting up, requires no software, costs very little to run and is a great way of monitoring your progress and linking what you're learning.

No need to be precious either about what your notebook looks like. Personally I'm a fan of Moleskine diaries (check out www.moleskine.com). I've learnt my lesson from regular abandonment of beautiful journals and notebooks that felt too nice to mess up with pen and ink. Writer Peter Hobbs found the perfect exercise

> ## Here's an idea for you...
>
> So pause for a moment and take a look around the room or space you're in. Choose one object as your focus of attention. Take your notebook (I hope by now you have one but, if not, grab some paper) and whatever form of writing instruments might be close to hand. No special pens needed. Without any more 'but I can't draw' comments focus on the object or scene in front of you and begin sketching or drawing. There is no right or wrong way of doing this – just focus on the curves and lines on the page.

books in a beachside 7/11 on the Gulf coast in Florida and describes the purchase as the best $2.98 (plus tax) he ever spent. Go for a notebook that's small enough to carry (Einstein kept a notebook with him even when he went sailing), easy enough to browse through, big enough to accommodate drawings and scrapbook mementos, and the kind of notebook you don't mind getting dirty. Let me know when you find one that fits that bill.

The easiest way to get started in your notebook is to do what feels right. Go on, give yourself permission to not only write but also to draw, sketch, doodle and paste. Yes, I did say draw or sketch. OK so the last time you did any drawing was back in primary school. Don't worry, these drawings and sketches are for your eyes only.

It's normal to think that the blank page just calls for words to fill it. But drawings and sketches can be equally revealing and insightful. Sketching and drawing not only slows you down, but also the very act of sketching helps you to notice and see things in new and different ways. Just the way you observe an object or look at a scene holds you present to that moment – and in that moment you are more open to listening and communicating with your own self in a much deeper way. It's amazing how much listening, seeing and noticing you do by keeping a notebook.

The notebook holds no limits. Good ideas that easily get lost in your busy day now get captured. It's a versatile machine, comfortable holding shopping lists next to ideas for a report, and to do lists, journal entries, observations and rants alongside reminders, of books to read, films to watch and music to listen to. Fill your notebook with pictorial evidence of your days. Or you might want to decorate blank pages with memorabilia like the ticket stub from the movie you went to watch last week. But be on the lookout for your notebook spewing out great business ideas hidden among the shopping lists and to do reminders.

But equally your notebook might be composed of scraps of paper, the backs of napkins or sheets of toilet paper (it's been done). Wherever you can plant yourself in words, sketches or doodles, do it. The Greek classical philosopher Socrates summed it up with this quote: 'The unexamined life is not worth living.' Thoughts not captured will wander off without you.

I cannot tell you how happy I am to have taken up drawing again. I've been thinking of it, but I always considered the thing impossible and beyond my reach.

Vincent Van Gogh in a letter to his brother

How did it go?

Q. Is it OK to continue with a journal I am already writing in?

A. I would suggest that you keep a separate coaching notebook. Many writers use a journal to deposit their feelings and emotions and then move on to doing writing practice in a separate notebook. This might be a useful model to follow. You can use your coaching notebook to gather thoughts and ideas about projects, work or your career.

Q. I have a habit of starting journals and then abandoning them. How can I ensure that this won't be yet another abandoned project?

A. One of the most common reasons for this happening is because we separate journaling from the rest of our lives. Disciplined and dedicated writers and artists aren't dedicated and disciplined because they're special. They know that they don't have to wait until they're sitting at their desks to write or that they don't have to be in their studios to paint. Their writing and their painting are with them wherever they are. British artist David Hockney is well known for travelling around London on the upper decks of buses and sketching. Now's a chance to make your notebook central to your life. It doesn't have to be worked on at a particular time of the day. Give yourself permission to write in your notebook at any time of the day. Little but often seems to work for many people. Make it small enough that it can slip into whatever bag you normally carry.

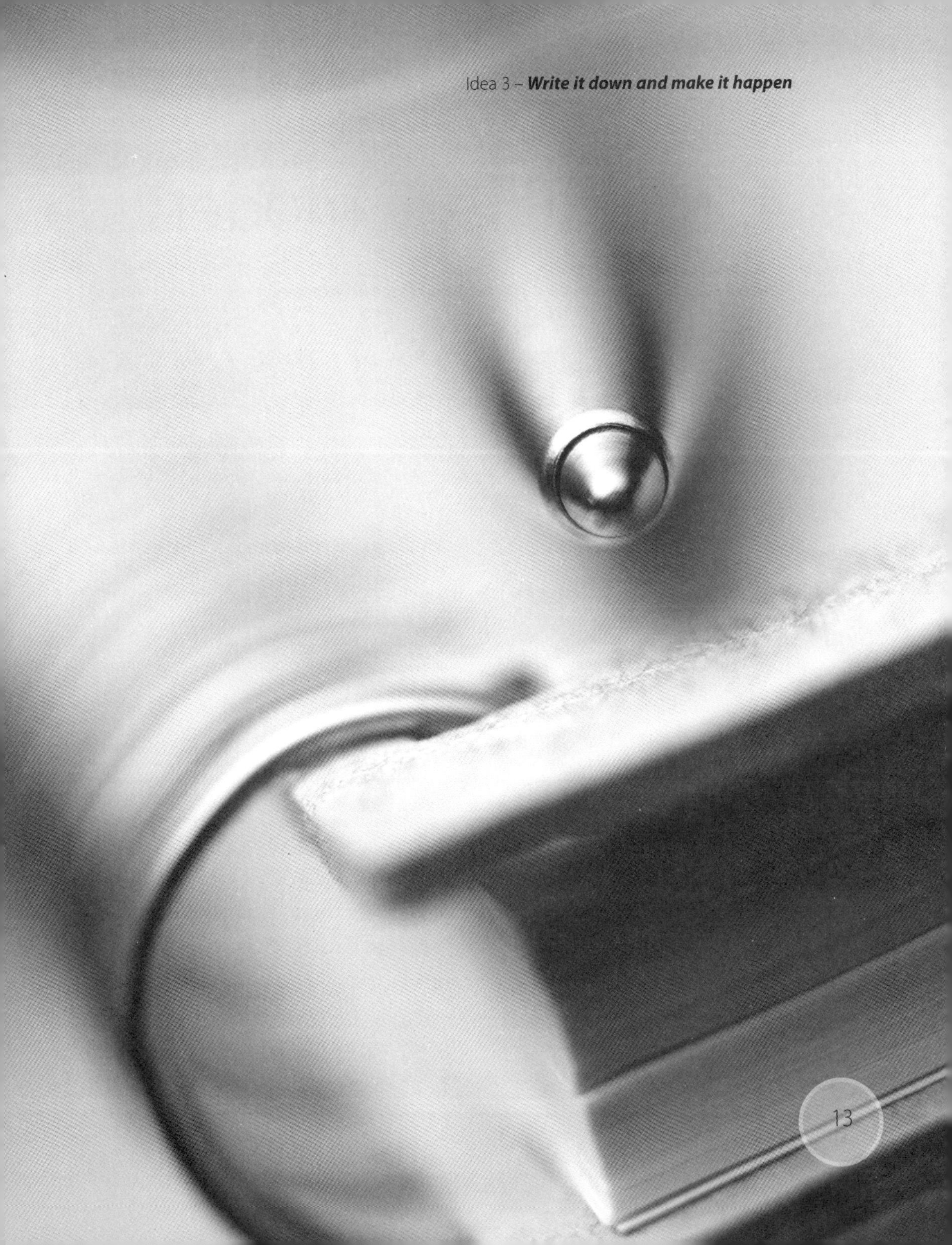

4. The CREATE model

Use the CREATE model as a path towards your success.

The CREATE model ensures you have a map for coaching yourself and a system that will help you stay on track. The model comprises the following steps:

- Challenge and create
- Reframe and replace your negative thinking
- Engage and energise
- Act and award
- Tools and techniques
- Explore and evaluate

Challenge and create

What challenges are you up against? You'll recognise challenges as those areas of your life that don't function well or where you feel drained or stretched. Once you face your challenges square on it's surprising how much better you'll feel. Whatever the challenge – drink, debt, a relationship, being disorganised (I've had challenges with all four) – at the very least be willing to tell yourself the truth. Why? Because once you own up to it then you can get on with the business of transforming it. Make a note of your challenges in writing. Without knowing how this will be achieved, take each challenge separately and ask yourself, 'If I had to create a different experience in this area of my life what would it look like?' Make a list of your new positive outcomes for each of your challenges.

Reframe and replace your negative thinking

Get into the habit of reframing and replacing your negative thoughts and beliefs. Say you find your inner thoughts telling you, 'Oh, you'll never be any good as a manager.' Interrupt these thoughts by asking yourself this question: 'Is this belief or thought moving me towards positive action or negative action?' If the answer is towards negative action then set about convincing yourself of the opposite. List all the reasons why you'd make a good manager and keep repeating these to yourself regularly and consistently. To reinforce the reasons write them down. Like your old habit, this new habit has to be practised rigorously and regularly.

> **Here's an idea for you...**
>
> Write a list of outrageous adventures you'd love to have. What would you have a go at? What would you try out? Where would you visit? What would you like to find out more about? Start off with a virtual adventure. Rather than the real thing be open to different ways of experiencing your virtual adventure right on your doorstep, through the internet, television, radio, photos, exhibitions, seminars, cinema, books or magazines.

Engage and energise

Start engaging with life right now, no matter how shitty it is. That means no excuses. If you just learnt that you're going to be made redundant then make a start right away on updating your CV. Don't make the mistake of waiting for your life to be sorted before you start having a good time. Get out there and enjoy yourself. When you start fully engaging with your life right where you are, you'll become energised, and so will your life.

Act and award

One of the most powerful tasks that helped put my life on a better path was learning to take action regardless of how I was feeling. So when I felt depressed I would still push myself to turn on the computer and send one email. The mere action of sending just one email motivated me to send another one. Once you get into the habit of taking action no matter what, build giving yourself awards and acknowledgements into the process. In other words, don't let your actions go unacknowledged. Today, what action don't you feel like taking that you could make a start on right now?

Tools and techniques

Do you have a toolkit of techniques and ideas that work for you? Your toolkit is a valuable resource in your journey to becoming your own best life coach. After several days of not writing in my journal during a particularly stressful time I noticed how disconnected and tetchy I had become. I took ten minutes out of a hectic day and planted myself on my journal pages. Instantly I felt better. Make a list of your life tools, the ones that work and get results, and use them regularly.

Explore and evaluate

Your journey to becoming your own best life coach is a chance to explore and experience life as the adventure that it is. Most of the satisfaction you'll gain will come from the journey itself rather than the destination. On top of this make a conscious effort to evaluate. Ask yourself questions, monitor your progress, record your achievements, make observations of how you navigated around obstacles and setbacks. Make sure you're a partner in your life and not an observer.

Is not life a hundred times too short for us to bore ourselves?

Friedrich Wilhelm Nietzsche, nineteenth-century German philosopher

How did it go?

Q. *I don't feel confident or able to tell the truth and to do all this work on my life on my own. Any suggestions about what I could do?*

A. Becoming your own best life coach is not a sentence in solitary confinement. In fact it's the opposite. What you'll find is that as soon as you start engaging with life, life will start engaging with you in terms of people, events and experiences. The path will be far from lonely. People with a positive attitude tend to act like magnets towards others. Value and make use of the people around you.

Q. *Am I expected to get order and balance in all areas of my life or is this really about me being a bit of a perfectionist?*

A. Balance and order in all areas is a tall order even for the most well balanced individual. Our lives are a constant work in progress, which was why, years ago, I named my company Life Work In Progress. Many people who are highly successful and satisfied in their careers and professions have been able to achieve this by focusing less attention on key life areas. So the writer spends less time on her social life so she can get her novel written. Sometimes imbalance in one area legitimately supports the balance and success in another.

5. Don't believe the hype

Negative beliefs won't magically disappear overnight. But is that any reason to believe your own hype? When you learn to manage and master your beliefs you'll be well on the road to even greater success.

When I was a young teenager I was determined to become a journalist or a teacher. Despite having really low self-esteem — the result of being sexually abused — I pursued both with a passion.

Even though on the inside I felt like shit I started securing slots on television and radio and by the age of 18 I decided to apply to train as a newspaper reporter. I sat the exam but wasn't accepted. I walked away from that experience feeling a big failure and believing that I wasn't good or smart enough.

Now even though my negative thinking didn't stop me fully from going on to achieve in other areas of my life, it placed huge limits on just how far I would excel with regard to my achievements. In most cases I would only allow myself to get so far before I would find a way of sabotaging myself or doing what Buddhists might call 'feeding the hungry ghost'. So I'd wake up early and get both me and my small daughter at the time ready, only to be late dropping her off at nursery and for work again just because I couldn't find my favourite lipstick. So no one was more surprised and terrified at the same time when I was headhunted for a senior management post by the chief executive of the local authority where I worked some years back. So terrified that my limiting beliefs kicked in hard and fast and talked me out of even sending off for the application form.

Now before you get too comfortable going yeah, yeah, I know just what you're talking about, hear me out for a little bit longer. Your negative beliefs are not all your own doing. Did you know there's a section in the brain called the amygdala that stores up a lifetime collection and memories of your negative experiences and emotions? A woman I was coaching told me she renamed this section of the brain Amy Gydala. The amygdala acts and makes decisions faster than the thinking rational brain, which tends to want to work out whether your reaction is substantiated or not. So, the amygdala gets a head start. Worried that you're under threat, the amygdala strikes out, wanting to protect you from further threat.

As soon as a negative thought or belief shows itself your job is to quickly scan your environment for evidence that will disprove it, even if you don't believe this evidence wholeheartedly. It will really

Here's an idea for you...

Get used to quickly replacing your negative internal dialogue with positive internal dialogue. Be neutral. No need to categorise your thoughts as either good or bad. Instead imagine a conversation that goes something like this, "I'm feeling really stressed out. Everything's getting on top of me. I think I'll take a couple of days off sick." Quick as you can replace those thoughts with a new response, one that is affirming and positive. So your new positive internal dialogue response becomes, "I will make some time today to organise my files and my notes. I will work on small parts of the project at regular intervals over the next few days. I'll make sure I take breaks and ask for help in the office." Repeat this technique as often as you can. Build up your thought muscles so that your positive self talk becomes a habit. You might not be able to change your external situation but you can change what you think, say and believe about yourself.

help if you write the evidence down. So let's say, for example, you're having problems believing you deserve to be in a loving relationship. Write down a list of times in the past where you have evidence of being in a loving relationship. This might have been a past relationship, or a relationship with a group of friends. Be very specific in your examples, which means naming people, specific times and places, and what they did. So write about the time when Tony (your ex) nursed you at home after a major operation. It's amazing what we will overlook when it comes to negative beliefs.

It is within your power to change your beliefs. On a regular basis make a list of daily or weekly achievements, no matter how small these are. The more evidence you are consciously connected to on a daily basis, the less power your limiting beliefs have over you.

Each morning we are born again. What we do today is what matters most. Buddha

How did it go?

Q. Can you be successful and still have limiting beliefs?

A. Yes you can, and here's why. You can activate and attract success to you while working on your beliefs. One of the quickest and easiest ways to do this is to act in contradiction to your belief. The limiting belief might still be there but by taking action you are actively eroding the power and hold the belief has over you.

Q. Is there ever a stage where one can get rid of all of their limiting beliefs?

A. Well I'm not sure about that one, simply because very few people I know of have ever reached that state. Certainly many people throughout the ages have reached a state of what one calls enlightenment: Mother Teresa, Mahatma Gandhi, Jesus and Buddha, to name a few. Whether they had limiting beliefs or not I imagine that it was what they chose to do or how they responded to their own personal limiting beliefs that made the difference. Don't forget the goal is not perfection. That's never achievable. I think we all have it within us to reach similar states of enlightenment. How long we can maintain that is what the journey of life is all about.

6. Question time

To bring about real and lasting change get into the habit of asking yourself the right questions. The right question, well formed and asked with clear intention, will point you in the right direction.

There is an art to master here. When you master the art of asking the right questions you're more than halfway there to finding your best answers.

I was halfway through a coaching session with a new coaching client when she blurted out, 'You scare me.' As the session progressed and we explored her statement together it became clear that what was scaring her was not in fact me (I'm harmless really – I promise) but the questions being pitched her way. One of the first things you will learn to do as your own best life coach is how to ask yourself the right questions and to coach yourself into a habit of self-questioning on a regular basis. You'll be developing questions that both put you in touch with what you really want and help in finding the best possible ways of achieving this.

Powerful questions not only change the way you think but also the choices and actions you make. You know when you've hit upon one of those questions when you think, 'Oh I hadn't thought about it like that,' or 'That's a good question,' or words or thoughts to that effect. Questions can be used to generate new possibilities and challenge old ways of thinking and behaviours, as well as validating and encouraging progress. But be prepared that when you ask the questions you're ready to listen to and take on board the answers.

To keep tabs on the kinds of questions you ask, use the following checklist as a form of accountability to ensure your questions are taking you in the right direction.

- Will making this choice take me towards what I truly want or will it keep me stuck in my past?
- Am I pleasing myself or trying to please others?
- Does thinking about taking this action make me feel energised or do I feel drained?
- Will this habit or action give me short-term gratification or will I gain longer-lasting satisfaction?
- Am I focusing on the solution or on the problem?
- Are my thoughts right now self-nurturing and affirming or self-attacking or critical?
- Will this habit or action empower me or disempower me?

Examples of questions you may ask yourself on a regular basis might include:

- What is it I really, really want?
- If I imagined that I knew what to do, the first thing I would do is?
- What solutions can I imagine that could solve this challenge?
- In a similar situation what have I done before that worked?
- If I had no choice but to make this work, what would I do differently from what I am doing now?

> ### Here's an idea for you...
>
> **Switching questions**
> Give the switching questions method a go. This method was originated by Marilee G. Adams, founder of The Center For Inquiring Leadership. Switching questions requires making the switch from the judger mindset, which focuses on problems and asks questions like 'Why wasn't I invited?' or 'Why doesn't she like me?' to the learner mindset where the focus is on solutions, choices and what's right and asks 'What options can I consider here?' or 'What can I learn from this?' Asking more questions from the learner mindset will create questions that focus on solutions and positive outcomes.

23

There will be times when a question causes you not only to pause but also to sit with it in your thoughts for a while. When this happens treat the question as an inquiry, a chance to reflect more deeply and allow the answers to emerge from inside you. Inquiring questions push your thinking below the surface of your everyday, mundane thoughts where you have greater access to deeper and more multi-layered aspects of your self and personality.

Finally, don't shy away from asking yourself the questions you'd rather not ask or be asked. You know, the kind of question that puts you on the spot or addresses an issue you would rather ignore. Bringing these questions out into the open can lead to powerful and often life-changing decisions.

Have patience with everything unresolved in your heart and try to love the questions themselves as if they were locked rooms or books written in a foreign language.

Rainer Maria Rilke, Czechoslovakian poet and novelist

How did it go?

Q. *I notice that I often start questions with 'Why?'. 'Why did I mess that up?' Why am I so dumb?' 'Why is that person better than me?' What can I do to change the way I ask questions that always seems to put me down?*

A. In coaching that is what we call a problem-focused question. 'Why' questions direct you away from your inner wisdom and from finding solutions. A useful method is to reframe and pose the question in the context of a solution. So the question 'Why did I mess that up?' becomes 'What did I do right or what did I do well?'. 'Why am I so dumb?' reframed becomes 'What evidence do I have of my skills and strengths?'. 'Why is that person better than me?' becomes 'In what ways am I different from that person?'. Reframing is a really useful technique that will help you gain confidence and skill in devising powerful questions.

Q. *How can I ensure that I am asking questions that will really stretch me and not just questions that make me feel comfortable?*

A. Go back to the accountability questions outlined earlier in this section. You can use any or all of these questions as a checklist to ensure that you are not just asking yourself safe questions. Another idea is to sit with a question in your mind for a while and to see what other ideas pop into your consciousness. Asking yourself the questions you don't want to be asked first will definitely point you in the right direction.

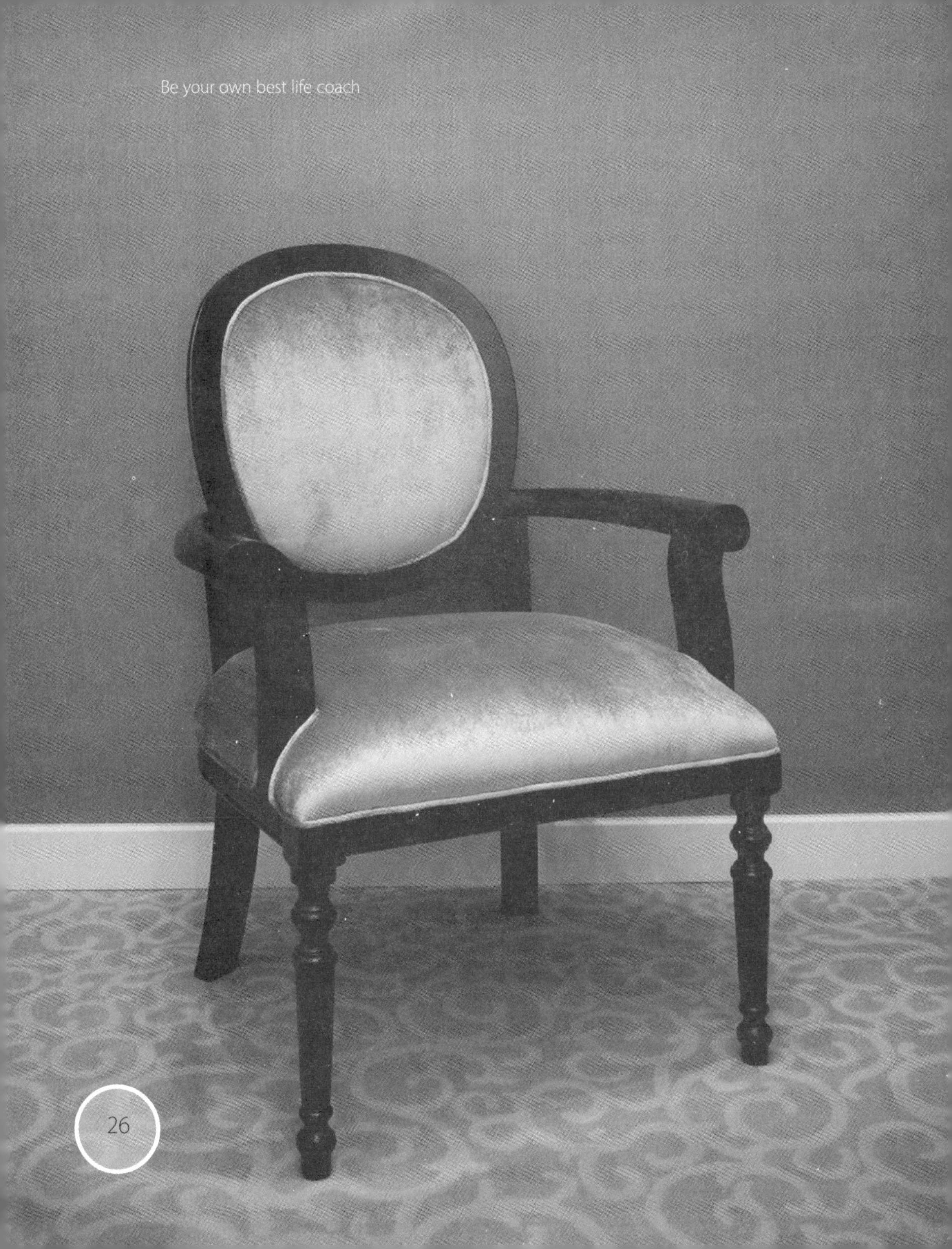

7. Don't talk to the hand, talk to the chair

Need clarity on an issue? Got no one to talk to? Ever thought about talking to an empty chair? Far from being a sign of madness, talking aloud can really help to clear the air.

People who talk aloud to themselves may be a lot saner than they've been given credit for, given the bad press over the years on talking to yourself. In fact they may have realised something that many of us seem oblivious to: that talking to yourself can in fact help you clear your head and gain clarity.

Years ago I went on a retreat where as a group we were introduced to the idea of talking to the empty chair, a technique pioneered by Gestalt therapist Fritz Perls. You may find this technique really useful when you have an issue to work through and no one to work it through with. In fact you may have people around but prefer to trust your own best thinking. I tried it out the other day. Sure it felt awkward at first. I had to make sure no one was around although my daughter and partner already think I'm a bit weird anyway. This technique really works when you have an outstanding issue to resolve. You'll need two chairs placed

Here's an idea for you...

Why not share co-coaching listening time with a buddy (someone who is a good listener and who won't bend the rules). You can do sessions face to face or on the telephone. You'll both get a chance to speak and a chance to listen without interrupting. Uninterrupted listening allows quality space for people to think for themselves. Once the first person has had their time talking, swap over roles and do the same again for the same amount of time. Listening without butting in, trying to fix or solve the situation or going off in your own thoughts is not as easy as you'd like to think. How about starting with five minutes each and then gradually building up your time?

facing each other. One will be the chair that you sit in and the other will be the empty chair that you talk to. Imagine holding a conversation with someone sitting in the empty chair who you're either in conflict with or need to make amends with. It doesn't have to be a person. It could equally be an issue you need to resolve.

Now you're going to have a two-way conversation with the chair. I know it seems a bit weird but hopefully you're alone with no one watching or judging you. Start off by talking to the issue or the person in the empty chair. Tell them what you're thinking and feeling. Once you have spoken shift over to the empty chair and assume the position of the person in the other chair and speak for the person or the issue. What are their thoughts and feelings? Notice if you begin to have greater empathy for the person. Having this type of conversation will help you clarify your feelings about and understanding of the person or issue.

Shift between the two chairs as often as you like, knowing that you are safe to express yourself in this moment, free from any retaliation and rejection. You'll also find that participating in this exercise gets you to take responsibility for the issue. You're not just leaving things to fate. Now you're actively doing something about it.

Really tune in and listen to the sound of your own voice. It's rare in our busy and noisy society that we get time to really hear the sound and vibration of our own voice. Is there heart in what you are saying or feeling? Do you need to speak some more? Are you beginning to understand things from the other person's perspective? Is this helping you bring closure on the issue? I'm sure you'll agree that there's often a big gap between listening to your thoughts inside of your head and hearing them spoken aloud.

Think about the issue you want to talk about. It might help if you give yourself a script, state your intention and allow space for pauses (remember good stuff happens in between the pauses but don't allow them to go on for too long). This is some of the best coaching you can get, certainly the cheapest, and best of all it will teach you how to capture and act on some of your clearest thinking. Give yourself a chance and you'll come up with some of your best solutions.

Who is not afraid of pure space ... that breathtaking empty space of an open door?

Anne Morrow Lindbergh, in *Gift From the Sea*

How did it go?

Q. I can't see how talking to an empty chair is going to improve my thinking. What research has been done to prove that this approach actually works?

A. There have been some recent small studies that suggest that the empty-chair technique is effective. But there does need to be lots more. Why not give it a try? Once you have a go you'll see that the chair is not the real focus – it's the talking aloud that will provide the real experience. Why not replace the chair with a cushion or another object that feels right.

Q. I'm not sure I've got anything in my head to talk about. What do I do if I go blank?

A. Treat going blank in the same way you would a pause or a silence in a two-way conversation. Most of us rush to fill the silences in our conversations. Our minds are so crowded with stuff that we need to give the mind time to empty. In that pause your mind is still working on accessing information. Why not sit with the silence and see what happens?

8. The Tao of goal-setting

What sort of goal-setter are you? Do you write a goal down or do you just move into action?

Do you want to know how to set goals that move you into action without putting yourself under undue stress or high expectations?

When I first started long-distance running I was overweight, depressed and had just come out of a long-term relationship. I don't say this light heartedly as up until then (which was around seven years ago) the only kind of running I had done was back in secondary school. But sometimes a goal catches you by surprise, catches you off-guard – but ready. It's had enough time cooking and it's ready to be acted on. You just have to trust your gut instincts on some things. When it came to running, my body knew that I was ready to take the plunge. You'll know when these goals show up because they'll be easy to carry out, they'll feel right and often they're the kind of goals you feel motivated to act on. At the end of the day some goals don't need words – they need action.

On the other hand, I'm also a fan of lists. I've made lists for just about everything in my life and amazingly have achieved many of the goals on the lists. Years before my running took off, and prompted by a course I'd attended, I wrote a list of what I wanted in a relationship (really wanted, not the superficial stuff). I was at

Here's an idea for you...

In the movie *The Bucket List*, Jack Nicholson and Morgan Freeman both play characters that are terminally ill with cancer. The presence of cancer in their lives leads them to create a bucket list – a list of things to do before you die. In the film Freeman and Nicholson focus their list on goals and dreams that both had denied or suppressed during their lives before cancer. But you don't have to wait until the onset of a life-threatening illness. Set aside some quality time and create a bucket list of your own. Allow your goals to be as outrageous and as wild as you want and as small and as personal as feels right. Now put that list away somewhere safe and get on with your life. Your list will take care of itself.

a point in my life when I had given up hope of finding a life partner. I was no longer desperate but open and very peaceful (seems this is one of the most effective places to make your goals and write your lists from). I'm sure you know that place where all that could have gone wrong had gone wrong; you'd survived to find yourself in that place of contented non-attachment. That's when the list started working its magic. When it creeps up on you unexpectedly, bearing gifts. Weeks later my new partner turned up and we've been together (OK, give or take a few choppy years) for over seventeen years. Grab your notebook and start making your own lists.

I'm sure you've also had the experience when, everywhere you look, you see the very thing you've focused on getting. I do this all the time with cars. Once I decide I'd like a car, I start seeing it everywhere. Is this just a fluke? Not really. Because there's an actual area in the brain called the reticular activating system that filters out 99% of your sensory input, allowing you to only see what is relevant to you. When you think about something you really want that message is sent to the brain. The brain then gets to work to materialise what you want, to bring it into your focus. A list anchors that focus in black and white.

So in my mind there's no doubt that writing goals down and writing lists does help to manifest your goals. But equally successful is the action of just doing it. I can't say that one is more successful than the other. But when we write down goals and lists and take actions that come wholeheartedly from our inner essence there just seems to be a different charge in the air that brings our desires – sometimes almost miraculously – into fruition. Go on, stop right now, take a deep breath, close your eyes and wish away.

What you get by achieving your goals is as important as what you become by achieving your goals. Zig Ziglar, motivational speaker

How did it go?

Q. I just seem to move from one goal to another. I don't seem to value any of them. What can I do to appreciate my goals more?

A. First off, have you made a list of all the goals you've achieved over the last year? Seeing your achievements in black and white is an instant confidence booster. Clients are often surprised by how much they've done and how much they forget. What about quarterly appreciations? Schedule time out in your local café or grab your notebook and head out into nature and take half an hour to review and appreciate the last three months. You'll start to feel more connected and appreciative of your goals when you make time to consciously acknowledge your achievements with small rewards and treats. Not taking this time is robbing yourself of your hard-earned successes.

Q. I find it really hard to set goals that aren't material or status related. Any tips?

A. What about setting some fun goals? Make a list of the activities that bring your inner child out to play. I love playing board games or buying an ice cream from the ice cream van (we still have them where I live). Ask yourself an inquiry question like, 'If I had all the material things I wanted in my life, what other things would I now love to have, be or do?' Keep asking yourself this question over the period of a month and recording the answers and thoughts in your notebook.

9. Small is the new big

Thinking small is the new way of thinking big. At the heart of every action, whether large or small, is a series of tiny, tiny steps that will have to be made to complete the task.

Smaller actions regularly executed make your job a lot easier than you think. It's far easier to manage a bigger goal or project that is broken down into manageable bite-size chunks than one that isn't.

How many tasks and projects have gone unrealised because you failed to break them down?

Approaching your work and tasks by taking small steps and applying minute incremental actions works particularly well when you have a tendency to procrastinate, are feeling stressed or overwhelmed, you're a perfectionist or you're afraid of failure. If you feel yourself resisting the small steps you've set yourself, break the steps down even further. The easier the steps, the more likely you'll be to complete the task.

I applied this technique with the first draft of this chapter. First I wrote the opening statements. Then I tinkered on the page with some thoughts. Then more thoughts came and before too long I had amassed 600 words. It all began with the first few words on the page and taking smalls steps along each line.

A micro movement is a very tiny action that's five seconds to five minutes long. A ten-second task is far easier to carry out than one that we know might take us five hours. Draw a blank circle and write the name of the project or task you need to complete in the centre (it's a good idea to choose one you've been avoiding). Divide your circle into several sections and label each section with the micro movement that needs to be taken. Date and time each movement, which can be changed. Work on one micro movement at a time. Prove a point and complete one of your micro movements in the next five minutes

Taking this approach on board will afford you time in your schedule to be inspired. It's inspiration that will spark ideas, generate and guide you towards creative research, heighten your observation skills and point you in the direction for right information.

Doing little but often allows room for ideas to ripen, like compost, affords you more space to make mistakes, abandon current drafts and the confidence to start again.

It's no wonder though, what with so much pressure to focus on results and performance, that we push ourselves harder and harder to value the big stuff. And, of course, sometimes tackling big chunks of a task or project makes absolute sense. The idea is not that taking small steps should be the only approach. One of the things you'll get wise on is knowing what approach will be most effective in getting the job done.

A few years ago I ran a journal-writing workshop. The participants – all women – complained that they didn't have the time to keep a journal. So I set them all a challenge in that moment. I gave them seven minutes in the workshop to simply sit and write in their journals. I wanted to prove that they didn't need a vast amount of time and that there really was value in starting off small. The response was amazing. They were blown away by how much they were able to get down on the page in that small amount of time and, most importantly, how those seven minutes had left them feeling. Many of them found that they wanted to continue writing. And here's an interesting thing about when you start small: you often get carried away in the flow and end up wanting to do more.

Have you noticed that it's the small things that make a difference in your relationships? I often make a point of thanking people for some small thing they've done. The impact is always appreciative. At work what small things can you do to make a difference in your connections with others? Something as small as a smile can make a huge difference. Could you make it a habit to send a 'thank you' after a project's been completed? Think about the small ways in which you can make a difference all round.

Writing a novel is like driving a car at night. You can only see as far as your headlights, but you can make the whole trip that way.

E.L. Doctorow, American novelist

How did it go?

Q. I'm a fast worker and always deliver on time. But there have been a couple of occasions where I've had to go back and amend mistakes or do things I've overlooked. What would you suggest I do in the future to avoid this?

A. You haven't said how long you allocate to your projects. But from what you've said my hunch tells me you haven't given yourself enough time for inspiration and the space for mistakes to emerge or enough time to notice where you can improve on original suggestions. Building in this time is crucial. You can still work fast but in between tasks let things sit for a while. This approach can work in your favour.

Q. I sent an email to a colleague the other day, thanking them for something they said to me, and they didn't even reply. How's that for focusing on the small stuff? Shall I leave it or get in touch?

A. Let me offer you another perspective. Two coaching clients in one day told me they had over 200 emails in their inboxes, most of which haven't even been read and won't be read any time soon. Either your colleague hasn't read your email or they've been meaning to get back to you but simply haven't found the right moment. How about sending a follow-up email? I'm sure in time they'll get back to you. Lose your attachment to your expected outcome or response. Keep to your word and your end of the bargain. That's what really matters.

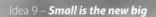

10. Bitten off more than you can chew?

Got too much to handle? Having problems keeping on top of your work? Here's how to prioritise so you can spend more time on the things you really want to do.

In an ideal world most people would love to prioritise tasks and projects based on what they deem as important. But in real life most of us, myself included, operate in the opposite way.

We do what time management and life coach Mark Forster suggests and prioritise based on urgency, which falls down to the fact that we don't give ourselves enough time to get tasks completed on time. I know I can't be the only one feeling guilty here as it happens to the best of us. But I bet, like most people, you'd love to know a way out. I'm afraid it's not good news. Chances are that what you're about to hear you've heard before, and no doubt you'll hear it again. But do bear in mind that the intention behind the repetition is to help you coach yourself to stop sitting on your work until it becomes urgent so you'll be able to eradicate the feelings of stress and urgency from your workload.

One way to avoid the stress of having to prioritise in the first place is to get on top of handling a task or project as soon as you receive it. So let's say you have a report to produce in one month's time and you want to avoid getting to a place where writing the report is deemed as urgent. What I'd suggest is taking the approach of getting started on the report almost right away. This is not something to think on but rather to do. So the request for the report comes in via an email. Within the next 24 hours find a space in your day where you can grab 15 minutes and brainstorm a list of the contents of the report. The next day you might write a rough draft of the introduction. On day three you might spend half an hour researching an area of the report. Keep this approach going over the next three weeks.

> ## Here's an idea for you...
>
> The next time you are given something to do, try under-committing by taking on less than you are capable of achieving and doing and then surprising people by over-delivering, by doing more. If you don't have the time to do more, you won't disappoint; if you have the time to do more, it will be an added bonus. Suddenly you'll raise both the standard and the value of what you deliver, but without the initial pressure of taking on more than you can handle. Not only will this support you in gaining a great reputation but you'll also be in control of both the quantity and quality of your work.

Obviously as you go along you'll put in more time, and that's fine, but you'll notice that you'll feel more in control and far less stressed. Producing work driven by a sense of urgency on a regular basis puts you in danger of producing work that's average and poor quality.

At the same time be careful of falling prey to allowing yourself to be dumped on by other people's urgent tasks. Tasks that have become urgent because they didn't act sooner. If the task can't be delegated it's within your rights to request the full amount of time you would need to complete the task. Get into a habit of saying no and giving the responsibility back to the other person. You could say something like, ' I appreciate that this is urgent but if I had received this two weeks ago I would have been able to take action on it sooner.'

Get a box

Get creative and take heart from the choreographer and dancer Twyla Tharp who starts every dance piece with a box. On the box she writes the project name and fills it up with each item that goes into the making of that dance. This includes notebooks, clippings, CDs, videos, books and photos. Over a period of time she places in that box anything that inspires her around the project. She builds in time for research, for reflection and allows herself time and space to experiment. Your box might be your notebook or a file on your computer. Or notes in a file. It really doesn't matter; what does matter is that you engage with it in a similar fashion to the way that Tharp does.

There's a difference between a work's beginning and starting to work.

Twyla Tharp, choreographer and dancer

How did it go?

Q. How can I know I am making the right choice?

A. What exactly is the right choice? A choice is a choice. Does it really matter if it's right? What matters is that you are taking action. Everyone makes wrong turns and decisions once in a while, but every time you make a wrong turn you get more information about what doesn't work and more opportunities about moving towards what does.

Q. I have a long list of tasks I need to complete in order to set up my website. When I look at the list my energy sinks. Do you have any suggestions of what to do first?

A. Start off by asking yourself this: If I were pushed to complete only five of these tasks, which ones would I select? Start with this task. At the same time, decide how you will get started. How about setting yourself timed sessions working on one of the tasks? It's common to overestimate how long a task will take when in reality less time is needed. Once the time is up, stop – unless of course you now find yourself in the flow and motivated to go on; then, by all means, give yourself absolute permission to continue.

11. What's your motivation?

It's a myth to think that you have to be in the mood to be motivated. When you know what motivates you, you'll be better equipped to call on those influences when you need them.

Here we explore some of the often-ignored elements of motivation.

Stay put

The discipline of staying put is one such often-ignored element of motivation. Regularly leaving my work interrupted my flow and the quality of my thinking. The longer I stayed put with my butt in the seat at the computer, the more motivated I became. Try it. Double or triple the amount of time you would normally allocate for a task and then stick with it.

Incentives

When it comes to motivation, incentives and bribes really help. Knowing you're going on holiday will motivate most people to get on top of their workload. The holiday serves as a short-term reward and incentive. At the same time, there's no point kidding yourself that you'll fit into a size 10 dress in 3 months' time for your sister's wedding when you're currently three dress sizes bigger. Pinpoint an area of your life where you would like to be motivated. Plan in smaller incentives that acknowledge your achievements and celebrate progress.

One of the best-known motivation theories was pioneered by American clinical psychologist Frederick Herzberg in the 1930s. This became commonly known as the two-factor theory as Herzberg identified two sources of motivation. The first category was what Herzberg named the hygiene factors. Included in the list of hygiene factors were the following: having access to supervision, opportunity for positive interpersonal relationships, a good salary and positive working environment. But his research identified that although the absence of hygiene factors caused dissatisfaction, they weren't motivating influences. The second category included achievement, recognition, work, responsibility and advancement.

Get to know your supporting motivating influences

What are the criteria or conditions that influence how motivated you feel? At a basic level many people are motivated by pain to move away from what doesn't work. Think about the times in your life when things got so bad you just couldn't bear it any more. Perhaps the pain manifested itself in your own life in the breakdown of a relationship or resigning from your job. The pain motivates you to make a change. On the other hand, it might be the incentive of a reward that you find motivating and encouraging. Even though I didn't enjoy many aspects of my Masters degree, the reward of achieving the qualification was enough to motivate me to complete my two years and gain the award. But it doesn't stop there. There are many other factors that have a strong influence on levels of motivation.

Here's an idea for you...

There are some tasks and projects you just won't be motivated to do. When this happens it's time to use rewards and bribery. Make a list of treats and rewards you enjoy giving yourself. Now make a list of tasks you feel unmotivated about tackling. Match one of your treats or rewards with each of the tasks you feel unmotivated to complete. Now take each item on this list one by one. You want to make sure that the treat or bribe is enough to get you going. When you read out the task and the treat that you'll be rewarding yourself with, notice if it resonates with a big Yes. If it's not a match, either replace the reward or bribe with a new one or up your offer. When it feels like a definite Yes, move on to the next item on your list.

What about power and authority? Or is your motivation enhanced by a real sense of belonging? What are the personal drivers behind your motivations? Tick the ones that apply to you:

- Power and authority
- Belonging and connection
- Achievement and contribution
- Rewards and incentives
- Praise and acknowledgement
- Deadlines and accountability
- Planning and being in control
- Fear of failure or fear of success
- Competition and proving yourself
- Inspiration and enthusiasm

Three of the most important social motivators are power and authority, belonging and connection, and achievement and contribution. Which of the three do you most identify with? Can you see the ways in which these motivating influences are being met in your current work and personal life right now? Acknowledging your motivating influences as needs that must be met is an important step to increasing how motivated you'll become.

I write only when inspiration strikes. Fortunately it strikes every morning at 9 o'clock sharp. W. Somerset Maugham, novelist and playwright

How did it go?

Q. I really dislike my job and want to look for a new one. I haven't updated my CV or applied for anything as yet. I've been feeling this way for over a year, so what's holding me back?

A. Let's tackle your CV. What is its current state? What needs to be done to improve it? How much time can you afford to spend each day working on your CV? Remember you can achieve a great deal by working in short bursts. But equally if you have the time, go at it with a blast. Give yourself a deadline with a reward at the end. Secondly, what do you like about your job? It's not a good idea to leave a job feeling this way. Make a list of the good things about your job, even the most obvious things. This will increase your level of motivation. No matter how bad a job feels, always aim to leave having acknowledged and appreciated the good.

Q. I find it hard to concentrate and this impacts on my level of motivation. I hop and jump between projects all the time. Any suggestions for curbing this approach?

A. None at all if it works for you. Some people are more effective working on several things at the same time. If you're completing projects and tasks on time then there's nothing to worry about. Don't forget, motivation will look different in your approach than it would for someone else. If not, retry some of the earlier suggestions in this section.

12. Please, Sir, can I have some more?

What we want and what we actually need fall into two different camps. Wants are desirable whereas needs are essential. The trick is knowing how to work out which is which.

If I asked you right now to stop and say aloud all the things you wanted, what would you list? A new home, a new car, more money, set up your own business, a relationship or a new job? Sound familiar?

Now think about this. What if I said today's your lucky day – your wish is my command. Now that you know you can have what you want, is the need to have it still so compelling? It's very common to find that the fact that you can have what you want means that the charge on getting them is significantly reduced and they're suddenly not that important any more.

However, getting what you want doesn't always make you happy, does it? Can you think of times when you have got what you want only to feel empty and unfulfilled days later? Think of all the celebrities with more money than you could imagine and yet they're still unhappy.

One of the reasons we feel this way is because many of the things we want only represent what we really want on the surface. Many of our wants are in fact driven by what life coaches sometimes refer to as unmet needs. For example, being abandoned by a parent may have resulted in an unconscious need to feel love and security. If this need is denied and not met in healthy ways then it may drive you to obtain the things in life you believe will make you feel loved and secure, such as possessions and relationships, all in an attempt to get this need met.

Take my former coaching client Gemma: when she finally lost weight she imagined that it would change not only how she felt about herself but it would also significantly change her life. The euphoria lasted for a few weeks and then it quickly wore off. By staying with how she was feeling Gemma got in touch with a deeper need that had been glossed over, which was the work she really needed to do on loving herself. On the surface her wants list included a slimmer body but behind that was the real need of loving herself. Once Gemma got to work on loving herself she found that she appreciated herself fully in a way that was not dependent on how she looked and other people's reactions to her body.

> ## Here's an idea for you...
>
> Imagine your house on fire. What items would you save from each room? The most popular items people save are photographs. Take a literal walk through each room in your home and make a mental list of seven items you would save if your home were threatened by fire (of course I hope this never happens to you). Now create a shortlist of three items you would save as a priority from each room. Are you surprised by your list? What you save is more about what you need than what you want. Today, what could you start letting go of?

Many people are surprised by how their priorities change once they start coaching around their needs as opposed to their wants. That's because when they begin the process of self-questioning it reveals the real needs rather than those you think you should want.

Needs are healthy and have a right to be met. When needs are met there is a general sense of relief and overall satisfaction that is absent in the presence of many of your wants. I promise you, getting your needs met will free you up to be the best that you can be.

Most of us don't value what we have. Instead we focus on what we lack.

Paul McKenna, hypnotist and NLP Master Trainer

How did it go?

Q. I'm a full-time mum with two children under five to look after and I find it really difficult to feel I have the right to even have needs of my own. Can you suggest a way to help me with this?

A. Motherhood is one of the most challenging jobs there is so I fully appreciate all of the pressures and just what it means to you. I also know that when mothers find a way to acknowledge and take care of their own needs they are better able to take care of those in their care. Would you drive a car without filling it up with petrol or oil? Well, it's the same. I want you to think about what really gets you irritated about your day or your life. Is it not having enough time on your hands? Wishing you could go back to school? Or wishing you had more time to meet up socially with friends? Think of three healthy ways you could meet each of these needs. For instance, could you organise a babysitter once a month? Or sign up for a weekend workshop at your local college? Work on meeting each need in a way that is healthy and nourishing and of very little cost emotionally and practically.

Q. I work full time in a director role in a large organisation. My day is chock-a-block with meetings and other responsibilities. I would love to meet a need to be more creative instead of spending loads of money listening to or viewing other people's creativity. Any suggestions?

A. If you haven't already, pick up a copy of *The Artist's Way* by Julia Cameron. It is a 12-week course in connecting with your creativity. You can work through it almost like a distance learning programme with most of the required writing tasks taking place first thing in the morning. If you've read it before, now's a chance to redo the programme again. Either way, enjoy.

Be your own best life coach

13. Get to know your values

When you've worked out what your wants and needs are, the next step is to identify what your values are. With your values intact, your life will feel like it is being lived with integrity.

To be clear about your values you'll need to have been clear on your wants, taken care of your needs and handled your tolerations.

According to Patrick Williams, founder of the Institute for Life Coaching, and Diane S. Menendez in their book, *Becoming a Professional Life Coach*, there are three kinds of values:

- The superficial 'shoulds' – These derive from the things we think we should believe and often originate in messages we have swallowed whole from parents, teachers, the church or some other authority.
- Chosen values – These are values we hold on to that resonate with us personally and we honour these values as consistently as possible.
- Core values – These are three to five critically important values that we have. When we are not upholding these values we're likely to feel dissatisfied, depressed, embarrassed or even ashamed. It's impossible to lead a fulfilling life that is out of alignment with our core values.

When your life revolves around your values, your values should add significant value to your life.

Here's an idea for you...

The Stellar Polaris is the star in the sky that remains in the same position. Many coaches and career professionals use this as a metaphor for finding your True North or Life Purpose. Your values are one set of tools that when honoured will point you in the direction of your True North. When you feel off track and your spirits are flailing, immediately schedule in that one activity, event or time with that one person or place that is guaranteed – no matter how much you're not feeling up to it – to lift your energy and put you back on track. Don't worry if at the time you don't feel like doing it; just remember that after doing it you'll be glad that you did.

Already you can begin to see how important it will be to steer your life in the direction of your core values. Let's say one of your values is respect and valuing what others have to say, yet your partner constantly interrupts and ignores what you say. You are therefore in conflict with one of your values.

One of the best ways to find out what your values are is to pose yourself lots of questions to find out what's really important to you:

- What do I feel strongly about?
- What standards do I uphold?
- What do I believe in?
- What are my rights?
- Name three things that I'm opposed to.
- What television programmes do I watch?
- What radio programmes do I listen to?
- What shops do I shop in?
- What magazines and newspapers do I read?
- What kind of music do I listen to?
- Do I prefer working indoors or outdoors?
- How will taking this job match my values?
- What values will be met by taking this job?
- What do I really, really care about?
- What do I stand for?
- What won't I tolerate in myself or in others?
- What career, profession or job would I do for free?

- What social/political/cultural issues do I feel strongly about?
- What's the worst thing I could ever imagine people thinking about me?
- How would I like to be remembered?
- What's original, unique or different about me?
- If I had a chance to speak out on a social or political issue, what would I speak out on?

After working through the questions circle key words and phrases that stand out from your answers and responses. There should be a natural buzz to the words that energises and inspires you. Pull together a personal statement using the key words and phrases that summarises your values.

For those of you with strong visualisation it might be helpful to depict your values as a huge jigsaw puzzle. Each piece of the jigsaw puzzle makes up an image of you from head to toe. Each piece of the jigsaw represents a different value so that when it is assembled it makes up all the different pieces of who you are.

All your life choices and decisions when in alignment are influenced by each of those values in different ways. This is evidenced in many ways, for example in the choice of which organisations you have worked for, what you stand for (or don't stand for) in relationships, and your social and political persuasions and personal boundaries.

Opening the oven doors at four each morning is like peeping into a treasure chest full of jewels.

Matt at Flour Power, Fresh and Wild's local organic artisan baker (Obviously Matt's someone whose job and values are clearly in alignment.)

How did it go?

Q. How can I make my values feel more relevant and personal on a day-to-day basis?

A. One way to keep connected to your values is to align your goals with your core values. When this happens there's a synergy between the two. The outcome of this can be habits and actions that support both the manifestation of the goal and the habit. Sound complicated? Well it won't be if you think of it like this: it's simply a matter of practising what you preach. Or some of you may relate better to 'put your money where your mouth is.' Enough said, I think!

Q. Is there an expectation that you keep the same core values throughout your life or can these change?

A. Yes, core values certainly do change and that's one of the important factors in deciding whether a core value is in fact a 'should' or superficial value inherited from your trying to live up to other people's 'shoulds'. As you separate the two you will be clearer on what your own core values are, which will shift and change as you change. What's important is to define your new core values and align these with specific actions, your goals and habits.

14. Put the past behind you

Ruminating over the past could be holding you back from enjoying both the present and your future.

When you've done the emotional work necessary, you'll be ready to put the past behind you and move on. No past is too terrible to move beyond.

In my time I've worked with a diversity of individuals including: women in recovery, chief executives and senior managers in the public and private sectors, media careerists and women serving life sentences for murder. That has meant listening to many, many life stories that at one end of the scale are full of achievement and success while those at the other end of the scale have been harrowing and heartbreaking, and some just seemed downright unfair.

Some of the events from my own past include being on the receiving end of physical violence and being sexually violated as a seven-year-old. However, when the labels, roles and circumstances are removed then the one set of things we all have in common is the often surprisingly shared aspects of our personal stories. But whatever past you've had (especially if it's one that's been traumatic) and whatever hand you've been dealt, I'm here to let you know that it's time to get over it.

Here's an idea for you...

If you're still feeling stuck and attached to your past, ask yourself, 'Who or what from my past do I still need to complete with?' Getting complete is a coaching term that's applied to either making peace or coming to some form of resolution with a person, event or experience. Make a start by writing down how you really feel in your notebook. If there is a person from your past that you would like to complete with but still find the thought of meeting with them face to face too difficult, how about writing them a letter that you never send? When you free yourself from the past you'll be free to move on to your future.

Am I being too harsh? I really don't think so. Why? Because I've seen too many individuals give over their power to a past that is long gone. Of course I'm not suggesting that this means overlooking the facts that you were wronged or mistreated. It simply means that you don't turn your energies into creating a lasting legacy to a negative past.

Reframe the past

One way to address this practically is to decide on how your past can become an inspiration for your future. Research has shown that when we are motivated to make choices as a result of past regrets it has a marked impact on well-being in later life. If you had to construct a list of positive consequences of your past experiences, what might they be? This means linking a negative event with a positive consequence. So for instance, you'd say, 'As a result of my mother dying I chose to ensure I raised a close and loving family,' or, 'As a result of having such a tough time at school I decided that I would become a teacher, a career which I have really enjoyed.' What regrets can you use as motivations to make changes in your life right now?

New endings

What about your giving your past a makeover? Like in fairy tales, why not give a period from your past a new ending? What characters from your past would get their comeuppance? Which ones would you replace? What would be your heroes or sheroes story?

Accept the nevers

Accept what existential psychologist James Bugental calls 'the nevers'. Make a list of all the things you will never be … 'never going to have children of my own … never going to be a best-selling writer … never going to be a millionaire'. Far from being pessimistic there's something comforting and disarming about embracing acceptance that leaves you free to embrace more of what you can achieve. What we may never be leaves more space and energy to concentrate our efforts towards the very things that we can be.

At the end of the day, the past has gone. What you're left with is the present. It's left to you to lay the foundations for your future.

It's never too late — in fiction or in life — to revise. Nancy Thayer, American writer, 1943

How did it go?

Q. I thought I had got over my past but suddenly, out of the blue, up have popped those intense feelings of failure. What can I do to move myself on again?

A. What did you do in the past that worked? Life is constantly presenting us with new challenges in different ways. These old feelings of failure may be around because you're about to take a risk or move into some new venture. I always find it useful to have a conversation with my feelings. Ask the feeling why it has popped up again. Convince it that you will take care of things.

Q. What do you suggest I do about my sister? We had an awful childhood but I've managed to turn my life round whilst my sister hasn't got over what happened to her. I've tried to help her out. What more can I do?

A. It's possible for you to love someone from a distance at the same time as protecting yourself and your space. In other words, your sister does not have to be a regular feature in your life. I know it might sound harsh but think about the consequences of letting your sister in. What are the costs to you? To help you through this keep a constant reminder of all the things you value and appreciate about your sister. Is there a way that you can keep contact to a minimum that would let her know that you still care and love her? At the end of the day get creative about how to stay in contact but at the same time be true to you.

15. If you don't succeed at first, try, try and then try again

Failure is a life skill that offers you information about what's working and what isn't.

Understanding the value of your failures can provide the stepping-stones to your success.

Here's a heartening story about a friend of mine whom I met at university in the early 80s. Back then she failed her driving test seventeen times and was finally successful on her eighteenth attempt. She came to pick me up the other day, driving the most gorgeous jeep. We had a little laugh at what it took for her to pass that test. But there's a real moral in that story: don't add up your failures; instead, take note of the number of times you were willing to try.

So, if you were to make an inventory of failures in your own life, what would make the list? Come on, don't be shy. Let me remind you that many of the world's greatest inventors, including Einstein, Isaac Newton, Lewis Latimer and Thomas Edison, experienced failure on a daily basis. Half of the goal of learning from your failures is owning up to what they are. Clichéd as it may sound, there is much to be gained from what failure reveals to us.

Here's an idea for you...

Here's your assignment. I promise you, you can't fail. Make an inventory of five significant failures and carefully work through each one, pulling out the reasons that may have contributed to things not working out. Look out for what went wrong. What was missing? What could you have done differently? What new opportunities were created? If you're finding it difficult to highlight the part you may have played then this is a good place to practise the 51% rule. Assume that for every interaction or experience you are 51% responsible. The idea behind the 51% rule is that by taking responsibility you will feel more motivated to take action and not be content with laying the blame or placing responsibility at someone else's door.

I coached a woman who lost a chief officer post and a social worker who was used as a scapegoat in a tragic child abuse case. Traumatic as both events were, both experiences opened new doors into lives which led them to what they really enjoyed doing. One of my former clients has now retrained for the Bar.

So what's one of your earliest memories of failure? One of my earliest memories of failure happened at secondary school. At the grammar school I attended every girl was expected to gain on average nine GCSEs. I walked away with two. I should have felt a failure but instead my results motivated me. I took the unprecedented step of turning my back on a year of secretarial studies, which would have been all that was on offer to me had I made the decision to stay on in the sixth form, and enrolled in college. That motivated me to work hard at college and I gained five more GCSEs in subjects that I really enjoyed. College was the making of me; I came out of my shell and formed new friendships. Along the way I racked up 3 A-levels and found myself at university by the age of eighteen. The qualifications that I gained after failing most of my earlier exams mean more to me because of the work I put into them. Failure offers a real opportunity on the other side to appreciate our victories.

In the event of a failure ask yourself the following questions:

- What wasn't working?
- What can I do now that is different from what I was doing before?
- What am I now free to pursue?
- What skills has the failure highlighted that I have?
- What part of my life has the failure allowed me to say goodbye to?
- What part of my life has failure provided new opportunities for?
- What victory did it or could it lead me to?

And always remind yourself what your biggest defeat has taught you.

Last night as I was sleeping
I dreamt — marvellous error!
That I had a beehive
Here inside my heart.
And the golden bees
Were making white combs
And sweet honey
From my old failures

Antonio Machado, Spanish poet

How did it go?

Q. I've been applying for chief officer posts in the Health Service since taking redundancy. I was expecting to have secured a post by now. Although I was unsuccessful in securing the last post I was interviewed for, they have offered me the post of Assistant Director. What do you think I should do? Shall I accept the offer?

A. Well it depends. First off, do you have enough funds in reserve to survive for another six months? Secondly, this may be a great opportunity for a number of reasons. You'll get to widen your experience, which will contribute to stronger applications in the future. This is an ideal opportunity to build and strengthen networks and contacts. Most jobs at senior and chief officer level are recruited through formal and informal networks. More promotions are awarded through sideway moves than direct progression. Use this time to prepare yourself for a future successful application.

Q. I tend to take failures very personally. Any advice?

A. I know changing this is easier said than done. A few years back I was encouraged to apply for a teaching position with an organisation I was already working with. In my mind, even though I was called for interview, I thought the job was mine. They gave the post to someone else. My first reaction was to take it personally. Then, on reflection, I asked for feedback. Turns out the successful candidate had a Masters degree in the subject. So, guess what? That bit of information prompted me to go off and complete a Masters, which I did. Since then I have been commissioned for two more major pieces of work with the organisation that I love. Feel your feelings for a short while but as soon as you can, get yourself back on track.

FINAL EXAM

SH LITERATURE

ND ANSWER THE FOLLOWING:

F

FAIL

d show one exam

65

16. The 'N' word

Learning how to say no puts you in charge, reduces stress and provides you with the valuable opportunity to speak up for yourself.

So what is it about saying no that causes even the most confident and assertive of us to take a rain check and find ourselves saying yes when in fact what we really mean to say is no?

We've all been guilty of it: inconvenienced yourself for the sake of a friendship, convincing yourself that at the end of the day you really are a good person. Tolerated being bored when you knew you would rather be at home working on your manuscript. Piled on the pressure and taken on more work than you could handle. So just what is it about saying no that makes even the most confident and assertive of us buckle under the pressure?

In one organisation I worked in, almost every week there seemed to be a collection for someone's birthday or leaving present. I began feeling resentful about giving to people I'd not even spoken two words to. So I started to say no. At first it felt awkward and uneasy. I didn't want to come across as mean spirited. But after a while my confidence increased, which meant that when I did contribute it was genuine and heartfelt.

Think of it like this: every time you say yes to someone else you're actually saying no to something for yourself. Over time your nos accumulate until soon you're building a wall between the things you feel you should be doing for others and the things you really want to be doing for yourself. These neglected nos are the stuff that kills dreams, erodes relationships and sees you spreading yourself much too thin.

Practise pausing

Before you next commit to saying yes or no, pause. Use this space to evaluate and decide if this is something you really want to do. Still confused? Then use a get out clause: 'I need some more time to think,' or, 'Can I get back to you?' Whatever you say, the golden rule is to get back to the person at your earliest convenience. The longer you take to respond, the higher the expectation will be of a yes.

Choose your response

When you're deciding on what response to choose, put to work the KISS principle. No, it doesn't mean landing a kiss on the other person's cheek. KISS stands for Keep It Short and Simple.

Tease out the benefits to you of saying no

When you say yes to someone it's likely you're saying no to something for yourself. It helps to stay connected to the benefits you receive every time you say a no in favour of your own priorities.

> ### Here's an idea for you...
> Some yeses are OK. You just need to know which ones. There will be some things that may inconvenience you a little but they may be so important to you that you want to make the time to say yes to them. Other yeses may have jumped out your mouth because you were put on the spot or you couldn't think of what to say. Count these as bad yeses. Ask yourself, 'Is this a good yes or a bad yes?' This will help you keep on track with what you're saying yes to and why.

Keep asking yourself this question throughout your day: If I say no to this request or demand, what will be the benefits to me?

No full stop is a complete sentence
When in doubt I always go back to a simple phrase my friend Doreen taught me some years back when we were running assertiveness training courses for women. Her exact words at the time were: 'No full stop is a complete sentence.' Make saying no a weekly practice. After all, saying no becomes easier the more you practise. Practising these tools will help you make better decisions about what you should be saying no to.

True success lies in deciding what our priorities are, and what trade-off we are willing to make.

Octavius Black, one of the founders of the Mind Gym

How did it go?

Q. My boss keeps giving me extra tasks because she knows I can deliver. At first I saw it as a compliment but now I feel resentful. Any advice?

A. Yes, I can see what's happening here. Although on some level your productivity and your enthusiasm have been appreciated you are now probably being taken for granted. Time to show your boss you mean business. Start by scheduling in an appointment to meet with your boss. Explain that the extra tasks – and clearly define them – are getting in the way of other important tasks. Request their help in re-prioritising your workload; that way you get them on your side. Then, if the time feels right, seize the moment – this might be the ideal time to initiate a conversation about reviewing your job description or even a possible promotion.

Q. My partner and I have decided that we want a wedding with all our friends and family but we don't want to invite children. The invitations have gone out requesting this and so far we have two requests to bring babies and small children whom we've been promised will be well behaved.

A. I totally understand you on this one and at the end of the day you just have to be firm. Some friends and family will try to test your boundaries. Still love them but stick to your original decision. It's your one special day and you have absolute right to set it up the way you want it. They'll get over it. For those who feel strongly about your decision, they'll make a choice about whether they celebrate the day with you or not. Hope you have a fabulous child-free wedding day.

17. Is your glass half empty or half full?

Your skill in interpreting events and experiences for better or for worse lies in your hands. Learn to nurture a positive point of view.

How do you interpret the things and events that happen to you? Even more important, how have you interpreted your own life events?

Have you ever contacted someone and heard nothing back? This happened to me not so long ago. Despite emailing a friend, three months later I'd still had no reply. It wasn't long before I began making up stories with all these awful reasons why the individual in question had chosen not to respond. Eventually, unable to contain my escalating anxiety, I sent an email pre-empting why I thought they might not have been in contact and basically trying to make amends even though I had no proof whatsoever that I might have done anything at all to offend. Talk about jumping to the worst conclusions. A few days later I received an apologetic email. Apparently I hadn't done anything at all. The long and short of it all was that life had kicked in: holidays, a death in the family and, oh, did I forget to mention this person heads up a centre employing hundreds of staff?

What was going on had nothing to do with me at all. It was my interpretation that was the problem. In a moment of unclear thinking my distorted perceptions based on previous experiences and assumptions were transferred to my interpretation of that experience. Just think of the energy wasted in second and third guessing. Energy that could well have been put to use in more effective and productive ways.

It never ceases to amaze me how siblings can all live under the same roof and have similar life experiences and all choose to view them differently. You're really not the product of your life experiences, or your thoughts and actions. Take a look around; you really do have plenty of examples of people who've had terrible things happen to them but have chosen to interpret these events in a positive light. My inspirations have included Maya Angelou, Iyanla Vanzant and Oprah Winfrey. All exceptional black women who have risen beyond being raped, abused, racism and attempted suicides to give the world the best of who they are. Take motivational speaker Wayne Dyer who was raised in an orphanage or Debbie Ford who got herself off drugs to become one of the USA's foremost coaches.

Here's an idea for you...

Think of a situation or event you would like to view in a different way and reframe this into a new meaning. What is your current way of looking at the situation? Next, think of three personalities that are part of who you are. These could be anything from the negatron, the hoper, the realist, the super positive or the joker. Imagine each of these sub-personalities as witnesses to your situation and that each will have their own take on the scenario. Write down each of the different views. Which perspective would be more productive for you to adopt? Just being able to see things differently gives you a new frame of reference.

Take a look around and identify your own models, the individuals whose life interpretations directed them towards a path of transformation rather than destruction. Remember you may not be able to choose the facts of your past but you can choose your responses.

Let me introduce you to a technique used by narrative therapists in supporting their clients to change the endings of their life stories. This is an extension of an earlier exercise. Choose an event in your life that bugs you or that makes you unhappy just thinking about it. Now decide on two new endings, for example as a comedy or good overcomes adversity, and rewrite this part of your life story. You not only have the power to change your script but also how you interpret it.

Life is not the way it's supposed to be, it's the way it is. The way you cope with it is what makes the difference. Virginia Satir, family therapist

How did it go?

Q. I'm always jumping to conclusions and assumptions about people or how I believe things are going to turn out and I'm afraid that I'm always right. The result often tends to be negative. What do you suggest I do to change the way I see things?

A. Well, you do have a powerful example of what happens when you think the worst – the worst happens. It certainly shows me one thing: that you're powerful in bringing about the desired outcomes that you focus on. When we look for what's wrong, guess what, we usually find it. What if you simply switched the way you think? For one week interpret as many events and experiences in your week positively. Even when it feels hard and it looks like the odds are stacking up against you, think positive. Keep track of what the outcomes are and, more importantly, how this new approach leaves you feeling.

Q. I'm in the process of splitting up from my wife and I am finding it hard to move on. Is there a way I can interpret this experience differently?

A. I'm sorry to hear about the split with your wife. To make the process empowering for you, why not write your wife a letter that you don't send? The focus of your letter will be on thanking her for everything you have valued about her and your relationship. This letter is more for you than it is the other person. Find someone you can trust who will agree to just listen as you read the letter aloud to them. Try to do this part face to face. Then burn the letter as a sign of you moving on. Good luck.

18. Secrets of the shadow?

Everyone has a shadow side, parts of our personalities and our character that we've judged as bad or not good. Normal instinct is to hide this part of our personality away from others and ourselves.

Doing the opposite and embracing the shadow may be the ticket to your emotional freedom.

No one's perfect. We all have parts of our personality that we tend to keep hidden. The challenge begins when we've attached certain feelings like shame and humiliation to certain parts of our personality and make-up. The trick is not to do what you've always done, which is to push the shadow self away. Instead I want you to practise facing your shadow, embracing it and then finding a way to integrate the shadow with the intention of reducing its overall charge.

These exercises will help you identify aspects of your own shadow and will help you to shift the focus and nature of your shadow self. It's a good idea to capture your responses in your journal as you will need to reflect on these exercises over time.

Johari window

Draw a large square and divide it into four equal-sized squares. Label the top left-hand box the public self; the bottom left-hand box is the secret self; the top right-hand box the open self; and the box below is the unknown self. The Johari window, a self-awareness model, was devised by two psychologists, Joseph Luft and Harry Ingram, back in the 1950s. The public self comprises the parts others know about us but we're not aware of. The secret self is what we know about ourselves that others don't. The open self consists of the parts others know and we know about in equal proportion and the unknown self represents the parts of ourselves we are still yet to know. The idea of the Johari window is to decrease the size of the public and secret self through self-disclosure and communication with others that will extend the areas of the open and unknown self. What parts of the secret self can you reveal to others in the next 24 hours?

> **Here's an idea for you...**
>
> **Coax your shadow out of hiding**
> Do you have a pet peeve or something that really irritates you? Let's say it's poor customer service in shops and restaurants that causes your blood to boil. What can you do to loosen the shadow's grip and integrate this part of your shadow? One way is to turn a complaint into a compliment. In the example of poor customer service you could go out of your way and consistently offer an excellent service where possible while, at the same time, appreciating and validating good service wherever you come across it in your own life. Write down an action that would get you started.

There really is something wrong with you

What about valuing and accepting your imperfect self, flaws and all? Everyone has flaws, from your doting parents, who in your eyes never put a foot wrong, to the mentor you credit for turning your career around. The problem starts when we judge these aspects of our personality as bad or wrong. Make a list of all your flaws and shortcomings. Be fascinated rather than frightened by your flaws.

Mirror, mirror on the wall

By not embracing the imperfect self you run the risk of turning the tables round and homing in on those very same traits in others. During a conversation with a friend she started complaining about her partner. Halfway through her complaints I burst out laughing. The very things she was complaining about in her partner were also true about her. What we deny in ourselves we often very quickly notice and dislike in others. Make a list of all the things – no matter how small – that annoy or irritate you about other people.

Individuals who are comfortable within their own skins are comfortable with all aspects of who they are. Your role as self-coach will be to continually find ways of bridging the gap between who you are in your private, secret self and the reputation of your public, open self. It may not be possible to ever fully get rid of the shadow but you can certainly change the way the shadow shows up and operates in your life.

Our job is to learn to embrace both the beauty and the beast within our nature.

Angeles Arrien, psychotherapist

How did it go?

Q. I have an awful secret that I haven't told my partner or even my closest friends about. Years ago I was caught stealing money from a neighbour's house. They caught me in the act but promised never to tell my parents. I still feel so much guilt and shame. What can I do to rid myself of the burden of this secret?

A. Well, first off, well done for sharing your secret with us. The more exposure you give your secret, the less energy and hold it will have over you. Secrets contain a lot of energy when they are withheld. Now what's the worst thing that could happen if you told your partner? The chances are your honesty may encourage them to share something similar with you, or it might bring you that much closer. I had a spiritual teacher once who kept reminding us that the more you can reveal your secrets, the less power someone else has over you.

Q. My secret self is full of flaws and things I don't like about myself. Is there really a way of even liking this part of myself?

A. It might be easier if you changed the word 'liking' to 'respecting'. Instead consider what your flaws may be offering you to learn about yourself. For example, being unkind to a friend might mean that you get in touch with the gift of forgiveness. Behind your jealousy might be a real desire to try out something new that you are envious about others doing. Respect the fact that your flaws may hold messages about what really matters to you while offering you real opportunities for growth.

Be your own best life coach

78

19. Pattern power

Are you aware of the patterns of defensive behaviour that you've cultivated over time that act as a form of protection against people, events or experiences that have caused you pain?

You may have outgrown a defensive behaviour but may be unsure of what you can do to change it.

Most people are familiar with the phrase 'becoming defensive'. You will probably have erected defences early on in childhood as a way of protecting yourself from painful or difficult emotions and traumas. Psychological and emotional responses and behaviours that may have served you well in the past and got you through childhood to adulthood start being less effective in providing the shield you once relied on. Your memories of your personal traumas and painful emotions get stored in a part of the brain called the amygdala, which also stores all your reactions to those experiences – whether you lashed out, froze, acted out in rage or became a victim.

Take for example Ade. Ade was let down by her best friend at school and as a result she appeared aloof and distant from other young women. By the time she had started working for a major corporation she brought her aloof defence pattern with her. The sign that her pattern and defence were no longer the protection she needed was when Ade was honest about the underlying feelings she began to have when she saw her co-workers waltzing off to lunch together

Here's an idea for you...

The next time you feel a familiar pattern kicking in, practise changing your response to the pattern. So let's say, for example, your normal pattern is to eat whenever you feel threatened or anxious. The feelings of anxiety and being threatened become your triggers. You defend yourself from the anxious emotions or the discomfort of feeling threatened by reaching for food. To break the pattern, interrupt the behaviour by inserting a substitute response. So instead of going straight downstairs to the kitchen, take a detour and head for your notebook and write for ten minutes about the feelings and emotions that have been stirred up inside you. For more support have a read of *The Writing Diet* by Julia Cameron.

and the realisation that once again she was left eating lunch alone at her desk.

So your first step in coaching yourself around your defence mechanisms will be to get clear on what they are.

- Think of three specific challenges you've dealt with.
- What behaviours or patterns did you adopt to cope with each challenge?
- On a scale of 0–10, with 10 meaning the defence still works well and 0 meaning the defence isn't working well at all, rate the defence in its current working order today.

Answering these questions requires self-honesty, a step Ade decided to take. She took time out to connect with the sadness and isolation that she felt underlying her defence pattern, and then she moved into action. Ade decided that once every fortnight she would invite a colleague out to lunch. Since this step was pushing Ade out of her comfort zone to buffer her fear of rejection she thought of the names of three people she would ask with the view of receiving at least one yes from the three possibilities.

Next step would be replacing the old defence mechanism. Together we decided to practise a visualisation that would offer Ade both a new form of healthy protection and inspiration for the new changes she was about to embark on.

Ade visualised herself having a great time out to lunch with her new friends. Every day she would sit at her desk and repeat the visualisation several times throughout her day. Soon she found she was not only looking forward to her lunch dates but each time she did the visualisation she was left feeling a sense of calm and peace that she hadn't connected with for a long time.

Within a month Ade had an active social calendar. She was enjoying work so much that she even planned a big lunch where she invited everyone to join her to celebrate her 30th birthday.

Feelings and responses that may have been appropriate in childhood may no longer now serve the needs of the adult. Learning to understand this will offer you the freedom to make changes and apply appropriate responses.

Defences keep us stuck in one unhappy place. It takes truth and courage to abandon them, but once we do, we discover a world of freedom and wonderful possibilities.

Dorothy Rowe, psychologist

How did it go?

Q. Can coaching help someone who has gone through a really traumatic childhood or am I better off spending time working with a therapist?

A. That depends. Each individual is different and each client has to be assessed on their individual circumstances. An experienced coach will inquire more about the work you have done in therapy and gain clarity about what they can support you with as a coach. By asking the right questions the coach will be able to work out quite quickly whether you're ready for coaching. A two-way conversation that is transparent should then happen between you both. I've worked with individuals who have returned to therapy because of an issue that has emerged from the coaching session and they've found returning really helpful.

Q. I made a mistake of letting my guard down by trusting someone and they let me down again. Wouldn't it have been better for me to have kept my defences in place rather than be hurt again?

A. This is a common experience. But there are no guarantees that you won't be hurt again. What's important is that you are clear about the changes you need to make to your boundaries to avoid this outcome as much as possible in the future. What limits do you need to set yourself when interacting with others? What do you need to speak up about? By keeping your boundaries in place you provide yourself with a safeguard, a healthy form of protection.

20. What to give up for change

One sure way to let go of the past is to learn to forgive. But forgiveness is not just about forgiving others. Forgiveness is also about forgiving yourself.

Things are going to happen that we don't like, are unfair or just plain nasty. When you forgive you make the choice to feel better about yourself and the things that have happened to you.

The moment her new manager took up post Fiona felt unsettled. Within a few months the cause of her feelings became clear as her boss started harassing and bullying her. At first she tried to pretend it wasn't happening. But when she found herself crying herself to sleep she knew this wasn't something she could ignore.

Everyone could see the strain and pressure she was under but no one dared challenge the manager who seemed to have a way of making everyone around her feel insecure. Soon Fiona started phoning in sick. She took more and more time off. When she did return to work her work standards slipped and before she knew it her contract wasn't renewed.

> ### Here's an idea for you...
>
> The Hawaiian forgiveness ritual Ho'oponopono is easy to do. Each morning bring to mind the person you wish to forgive. Close your eyes, take a few deep breaths and repeat the following words several times: 'I am sorry I hurt or offended you. I love you. Please forgive me.' Keep repeating over weeks and months until it eventually feels true.

I know what you're thinking: how unfair. And, yes it, was. It's so easy to not want to move on but instead wallow in self-pity. We've all been there. But we'll need to eventually pick ourselves up and face the music because holding on to any negative feelings about another person eventually hurts you and not the other person.

It did take Fiona a few months to process her anger and resentment. It was natural to feel hurt, rejected and unfairly treated. But finally we started exploring where she was at and what she wanted to do. When Fiona explored the options she decided that whilst feeling hard done by was a reality, on the other hand the cost of holding on to these feelings was far too great. Why not make a list of the benefits of holding on and the benefits of letting go. Seeing the benefits and costs in black and white brought things into sharp focus.

Fiona didn't exactly use the words forgiveness in our conversations but her actions and process certainly reflected many of the same and similar feelings others have gone through when sharing their experiences of forgiving.

By forgiving and letting go Fiona applied the brakes to her own negative self-talk. She forgave herself for not standing up for herself, for not reaching out to others and asking for help and she forgave herself for believing that she was helpless and weak.

Doing this work was crucial if Fiona was going to give herself a real chance of succeeding again at work and believing in what she had to offer.

Negative feelings about past events and people wastes valuable energy that you could be directing towards your business and your future goals. This is energy you are stealing from yourself. If the word forgiveness does not work for you, replace it with something else.

You know it's time to forgive when:

- You're harbouring resentment and bad feelings
- You find yourself blaming others
- You're caught up in a cycle of negative self-talk
- You feel tired and drained
- You're still attached to events and people from your past
- You're working hard and not getting what you want

At the end of the day forgiveness frees up your energy. You need this energy to get to work on your life.

Self-forgiveness

At the end of the day the most important person you'll need to forgive is yourself. Think about how many times throughout your day you beat up on yourself with your negative thoughts and beliefs. For the next ten minutes just close your eyes and bring to mind three things you would like to forgive yourself for. Hold these in your thoughts as you repeat them to yourself several times over. After ten minutes open your eyes and sit quietly for a few moments before you get on with your day.

Forgiveness is the fragrance that the violet sheds on the heel that has crushed it.

Mark Twain, writer

How did it go?

Q. I'm finding it really hard to forgive someone from my past. I know it has had an impact on my self-confidence and self-esteem and I don't want to let this person off the hook. Any advice?

A. Forgiveness is certainly not about forgetting or letting people off the hook. In fact, consider this. What if I said to you that the intention of forgiveness is in fact the opposite, to let yourself off the hook? What if you could free yourself from the emotional or psychological attachment this experience has to your present? Wouldn't that be liberating? When you forgive, you release the person from your emotional energy. Otherwise you'll be stuck with them for years to come.

Q. I find it much easier to forgive others than I do to forgive myself. Is there anything I can do to really get to work on forgiving myself?

A. I have given this exercise to many clients with remarkable success. It involves writing out an affirmative statement or mantra twenty-one times in your notebook every day for one week. Say you want to forgive yourself for not believing in yourself. Your mantra becomes a sentence that affirms your self-worth: I am worthy and lovable just as I am. Clients have fed back that taking the time to write the sentence out twenty-one times each day becomes a nurturing and validating habit.

21. Silence of the mind

To be really effective you'll need to create time in your day where you have quality time to think. So what can you do to make silence your friend and you a friend of silence?

I'm certainly no angel when it comes to making a bit of noise. But in public spaces there's a certain etiquette I adhere to in order to keep my own personal noise under control.

I keep to brief conversations on my mobile; after all, is it really necessary for half of the train carriage to know what shopping I need to bring in for dinner as I talk to my other half? I haven't joined the masses and invested in an iPod yet and I hope that when I do (there's a birthday around the corner) I won't inflict my choice of music loudly on to others. I'm resisting getting a BlackBerry after watching a friend who came to dinner check and respond to emails every ten minutes as she talked with us.

Not only does taking time out to be quiet and in touch with our thinking slow us down but it also puts us in touch with solutions that we can access far more readily when we gives ourselves time and space to think.

Take a leaf out of the life of writer Nicholson Baker and invest in a pair of industrial earplugs. Wearing a good pair of earplugs makes all the difference in reducing the noise of everyday sounds that invade your headspace. Suddenly noise that is right in front of you is pushed several feet away. The trick is to make sure the earplugs have a good seal. You'll know because when pulled from your ear you should feel a tiny prick of pain. Any more pain and I strongly suggest investing in a different brand.

It's not necessary to be alone to access your own inner silence. It's quite possible to feel alone in a crowd of people. In a group of people just close your eyes and feel yourself sink into your own thoughts. Try taking a few deep breaths and imagine sitting in the middle of a bubble that only you can enter. This is a good way of sealing yourself off and being in your own space. During a really hectic time last year I thought the idea of spending time alone by myself would be bliss. So when I was kindly awarded a two-week stay in my own cottage in a fabulous retreat centre in America I was ecstatic. What I hadn't banked on was my reaction to nature being my only soundtrack, two weeks where I barely slept at all. At night the quietness was unnerving. Arriving back home I really appreciated how much I also needed the stimulation of some external noise.

Taking time to be silent really does offer you a number of benefits. Over time thoughts become less self-critical and you'll generate deeper ideas and solutions as well as clarify your thoughts and your thinking. You'll notice how the thoughts and decisions made from this place seem to possess a greater clarity and possibility of working than thoughts and solutions generated in other ways.

Not surprisingly many of us resist connecting with our own inner silence. I think we do this because of knowing that we might not like what we find in that space. The more quiet time you carve out in your week, the less afraid you'll become.

It's a good idea if you find that your thoughts start to take over to set yourself five minutes of free writing into your notebook before you get quiet. This is a good way of emptying your thoughts on to the page. Write as quickly as you can about anything that's on your mind.

During a recent trip to a spa I had to speak out in order to claim some silence while I was receiving a treatment. That involved requesting that the music was turned off and that the body therapist stopped talking at me (of course I was very polite with my request). End result: I had a blissful treatment and enjoyed being alone with my thoughts.

Silence is the natural organiser. Laura Berman Fortgang, life coach and author

How did it go?

Q. I really find it hard to be still. I find meditating really frustrating. Could you advise me on what else I could do?

A. Love the question. I'm not good at meditating either, you'll be pleased to know. But when I run I always connect with a really quiet place inside myself. In this place it feels exactly like the places I can get to in a meditation. Other people swear by walking. I think that the mistake many people make is believing that somehow if they're not meditating then they're not being silent. I'd suggest finding whatever activity it is you do that makes it easy for you to connect with this place inside yourself and then find a way of connecting with it regularly.

Q. I suffer from mild depression and being silent seems to trigger it. Is there a way round this?

A. The way round it is to take the words of Buddhist and Zen meditators, among the most practised and experienced practitioners of meditation, and stay with the feelings and thought. Buddhists suggest employing the act of mindfulness. Let the thought come, notice it, and then let it go and bring your awareness and attention back to your breathing. Having suffered with depression myself I know how difficult it can sometimes be to stay with a practice like meditation. Don't push your thoughts away. Instead embrace them. It might be helpful to join a meditation class or learn from a qualified teacher. The Brahma Kumaris runs classes and workshops in the UK. You'll find them at www.bkwsu.com or www.brahmakumaris.com or try www.globalretreatcentre.org.uk. Your local area will have a range of meditation classes on hand.

22. When doing nothing actually pays off

So you find yourself missing deadlines, daydreaming or loafing. But what if procrastination is much better for you than you think? The trick is knowing when procrastinating is OK and when it's not.

I'm a recovering procrastinator who, by the way, still procrastinates. The only difference now is that I know when it's perfectly OK to procrastinate and when it's not.

I constantly remind myself that a little bit of procrastination is better for you than you think, and here are three reasons why.

Examine your deadlines

Don't be fooled by all deadlines. Some of the most important actions that move your life and your business forward rarely have deadlines attached to them. Many deadlines in fact lull us into a false sense of security. If a deadline's been set – whether by you or by someone else – that's either premature or not important enough, the mind knows it and so do you. In fact procrastination may be your inner genius telling you what to do. A deadline's not always an accurate indicator of what's most important to achieve right now. Your deadline might have been appropriate three months ago but since then both time and circumstances have moved on. It's important to keep a constant check on your deadlines to decide whether they're current or not.

What meaningful goals and commitments have you ignored that don't have a deadline attached? What if you concentrated your daily efforts on completing 15% of these goals and commitments as part of your daily to do list? That way procrastinating on the remaining 85% of activities suddenly becomes legitimate. Sometimes knowing what tasks to procrastinate on is a really good way of effectively managing your to do list.

How do you know when it's genuinely OK to procrastinate on a deadline?

- Delay's the right thing because there hasn't been enough lead-in time or the right amount of time for processing.
- Some things just shouldn't be done and you can't know for sure unless you've put them off for a while.
- You feel energised and not demotivated. You experience no feelings of guilt as a new date for completion is set. You can't wait to get on with the work at hand.

Put off planning

Ever noticed how too much planning early on in a project can result in you having to redo most of the planning along with introducing new tasks as the

> ### Here's an idea for you...
>
> Reduce the items on your to do list by assembling a 'things not to do' list. Ask yourself this: What activities could I stop doing from today onwards? Include both long-term commitments and small everyday actions. Bottom line is that your bed doesn't know when it's not made, the dishes don't know when they aren't done and you certainly don't have to be the one to do them. Your things not to do list is your passport to a streamlined life that includes more time and space for things you want to do but just didn't previously have the time for.

project nears completion because circumstances and events will and do inevitably change? At the start of a project, making notes (which are added to over time) and setting up a file are fine but planning too far in advance can sometimes mean setting yourself up for planning twice. So by starting your more detailed plans at the right time you're not only saving yourself time but you're also being more effective in your execution of the project.

Daydreaming and being idle are OK

Taking time away from your work and giving it space to breathe can be mistaken for procrastination, and we all have a tendency to label this process so. But it's necessary to allow time for recharging creative energy. While writing this chapter I abandoned the computer and did a spot of vacuuming. In that time my mind freely rambled around, examining the work and coming up with great ideas and suggestions for how to make it better. Connections and suggestions were made that I just don't get when I'm up close.

Believe it or not, when approached in the right way cleaning, shopping, eating, watching TV and even sleeping are valuable and productive stages of the creative process, allowing the mind to work away from the work. It's hard to conjure up ideas on demand. Some of your best ideas emerge when you're relaxed.

Procrastination isn't always a bad thing. It can keep you from working on tasks that ultimately turn out to be less important than you thought. Eric Abrahamson and David H. Freedman, psychologists

How did it go?

Q. How can I be sure that I am using the time doing nothing productively and not just as a front for procrastinating?

A. You're right, there is a very thin line. But I find what really helps is to put a time frame on time spent doing nothing. Sticking to your allotted time lessens the possibility of procrastination. So a twenty minute break has its place in your day but doesn't turn into a whole day away from your task.

Q. The idea of just sitting doing nothing sends me spare. What can I do to make this more of the pleasurable task that it should be and actually look forward to spending time without an agenda?

A. Very often entering a space of having nothing to do actually brings to mind all the things that we're unhappy about or perhaps avoiding. In other words we tap into worry and anxiety. The simplest and easiest thing you could do when these feelings arise is to close your eyes and take several really deep breaths. As thoughts enter your mind (which they will do) instead of judging them and pushing them away allow them to rise and fall away as you focus your concentration on your breathing. The idea is not to push your thoughts away but to follow their flow and let them go. Just a few minutes of this practice can be remarkably calming.

23. Help, I need more time

Want to know how to free up valuable minutes in your day? You can't increase the number of hours in a day, but you can get more from the time that you have by changing the way you use it.

Are you faced with too much to do and not enough time? I'm no time management guru but over the years I've become smarter at eliminating the time-wasters from my day that led to poor time management.

Time is probably one of the most coachable issues that we work with. We want more of it and we want to know how to tame it. I might not have all the answers but here are five simple approaches I've used that will help you free up valuable minutes – even hours in some cases – throughout your day. But be warned: they only work when rigorously applied.

Track your time
Try tracking if you're often late or miss appointments. Over the course of one day time as many of your daily activities as possible. Tracking your time may quickly

reveal some startling truths. After completing this exercise one of my coaching clients realised that what she thought was only one hour checking her email each day actually amounted to three. She was able to reduce this time significantly and as a consequence got more done.

Hire in help

Ever had the feeling that your to do list is never ending? The volume of routine tasks on your to do list may seem harmless but these tasks steal time from the important things. If you could afford it, what activities would you pay someone else to do? Is there a way to start with the least inexpensive activity and hire someone straight away? Can any of your tasks be delegated? Or is there a need to make a decision to stop doing the activity altogether?

Mobilise the time you have

This is particularly important when you have a limited amount of time to complete an action. Have you had plenty of time to meet a deadline and instead found yourself distracted and wasting time? Or maybe you're up against a tight deadline to get a task completed that would on a normal day take double or triple the amount of time? Suddenly you're on top of it. You pull out all the stops and in the time you have the job gets done. You've just experienced what time management gurus refer to as Parkinson's Law. Parkinson's Law can be effectively

Here's an idea for you...

Put yourself on a media fast and reclaim valuable minutes and hours lost throughout your week. Fast for as little as an hour or up to 24 hours or more. No need to go cold turkey. Simply decide on what media aspect you will take a break from. Will it be television, radio, texts, emails, the internet, the computer, reading subscribed mail-outs, newspapers or magazines? The good news is that your fast can be broken and restarted when and as you like. Use the time gained to focus on activities and tasks that really matter. Or just simply relax.

used in both scenarios by setting aside a certain amount of time that you stick to while you concentrate your focus and get the task completed in the allocated slot of time.

Strategic deceit

This is very useful when it's a challenge to schedule in me time. Fabricating self-imposed meetings and appointments in your diary is another way of saving time. Writer Heather Sellers calls this 'strategic deceit'. It's not the same as lying but a method used to create time that you wouldn't normally allow yourself to have. What harm would it really do to schedule in the end of a meeting an hour later so you can take an uninterrupted lunch break before rushing back to the office? You're more likely to give yourself permission to make time for yourself when you've scheduled it in your diary in the same way you schedule in appointments for clients and other people.

Intelligent neglect

A simple time analysis may reveal the fact that you're spending far too much time on your computer or your mobile phone. Spending less time on the internet or your mobile phone (even small chunks of time) lowers stress and allows time for reflective thinking and solution solving. Time to think increases productivity and efficiency. In the time management world taking time off from technology is known as the practice of 'intelligent neglect'. It includes regular periods of switching your mobile to voicemail, going through your inbox and unsubscribing from mailing lists, and checking emails only once or twice a day.

Your greatest resource is your time.

Brian Tracy, entrepreneur

How did it go?

Q. My to do list goes on for ever. What can I do to get me off this never-ending treadmill?

A. The thing is your to do list can be as long or as short as you want it to be. Ever thought of making a shorter to do list? Each night write down no more than three to five actions that you want to accomplish the next day. Achieving five out of five is more satisfying than five out of twenty. You'll probably always get most things done and even end up with the possibility of doing more. To top it off, any other completed actions from the remaining fifteen items become an added bonus.

Q. The demands of my job and a young family make it impossible to find time to exercise. Isn't it better for me to accept that the time's just not there?

A. If you're willing to look hard enough at your life and where your time is going, I bet you'd find the time, no matter how little, to exercise. I came across an old magazine the other day that reminded me how three women found time to exercise despite extremely busy schedules: One combined exercise with another activity, like walking the children to school instead of driving. Another replaced a household responsibility with exercising, which required delegating the duty to someone else, and the third convinced herself that she would only exercise for ten minutes and then found she exercised for much longer than she had intended.

24. Free time

Can you find 15 minutes in your day that would count as free time? If the answer is no then you need to do something about it right now.

Does the idea of having free time feel like a double-edged sword? We dream and talk obsessively about it and then when we get it we either twiddle our thumbs or find ourselves filling the space with some other mindless activity.

We're more haste and speed than ever before, filling every second of our day with something to do. All of this begs one question: Just how comfortable are you with the idea of free time and are you making the best use of it?

Take a look back over your schedule for the last six weeks and note down the last time you had time to yourself. Did your time out have to be dragged out of you because it was a Bank Holiday and you were staying with your in-laws in the country? Once it was there how did you use it? Did you make the most of it? Or did you waste it away? Whether it's making the time or how you use it, here are three simple approaches to getting the most out of your free time.

Think necessity, not reward

Many people treat free time as a reward for hard work. And you know, we're pretty bad at rewarding ourselves, certainly in any conscious way. I'm going to suggest that you think of free time in a different way. Think of your free time as a preventative activity rather than a reward. Free time is one way to build reserves, generate ideas and solutions and to get into a frame of mind where you can access some of your best thinking. You'll not only need lots of free time that is connected to rewards but also free time that is firmly fixed to healthy well-being. Don't wait until you're burnt out to bring free time into the centre of your schedule.

First things first

Booking free time as you would any other appointment in your diary is one way of protecting your free time and ensuring that it happens. Make free time a priority by scheduling free time first, before any of your other appointments. I know you're probably thinking, why didn't I think of that? It's a good idea, isn't it? This way your free time doesn't get tacked on the end somewhere with the likelihood of it being bounced off the schedule by other pressing engagements. Not only that but you've immediately sent yourself the message that putting this time first in your diary means that it's really important to you.

> ### Here's an idea for you...
>
> Everyone deserves a room of their own. But it doesn't need to be an actual room. One friend's room is on wheels – her car. Another takes refuge in her library room, the pages of her journal. One year my room was outdoors, underneath the branches of a huge oak tree. When he first came to London, poet, novelist and broadcaster Benjamin Zephaniah's room was a bench on a roundabout in Stratford where he would sit and watch the world go by as he figured out how to sort out his life. Whether in public or private, mark out your room of your own and schedule in a time to visit it in the next seven days.

Know the first thing you're going to do

Give yourself something to do in the first ten minutes of your free time. I know that sounds weird but this way you're more likely to stick with it than fill the space when you feel bored or restless doing something else. Say you've got a two-hour slot and nothing planned. If you sit there doing nothing at all your busy mind will simply suggest loads of things you could be doing. Before you know it you're making a few phone calls and checking your email. Instead plan activities that will focus and centre you but not take you away from your free time. You could spend ten minutes meditating, going off on a ten-minute mindful walk or spend ten minutes writing in your notebook. It might seem like it's going against the grain but these activities will ground and support you to make the most of your free time whenever you have it.

Much of the day should be in a strict sense idle, for it is often in idle moments that real inspiration comes. John Updike, novelist

How did it go?

Q. Are you saying that I should stop what I'm doing and have some free time?

A. Yes and no. It might be more beneficial to finish the current thing you're working on, especially if you are near completion. But certainly I would advise you to build regular free time into your schedule regardless of how busy you are. This is not about luxury. This is about necessity. Your free time contributes to your productivity. Push yourself without breaks and you're not getting the most out of you. It's one of those things where you have to take the action first before you really feel the benefits. Start off with ten minutes' free time and gradually build up more time.

Q. I tried scheduling in free time first but because I knew it could be moved I shifted it at the last minute. How can I prevent this from happening again?

A. You might need to do something more to establish this appointment as unmovable in your schedule. Time management coach Mark Forster suggests tricking the reactive mind by lying to it. This is possible because the reactive mind can't tell when the rational mind is lying. So you could say something to yourself like, 'I'm only going to meet with myself for five minutes.' That way you take the first step even though you have two hours scheduled into your diary. The first step will be less of a threat to the reactive mind so it won't resist. Next thing you know, your two hours has flown by.

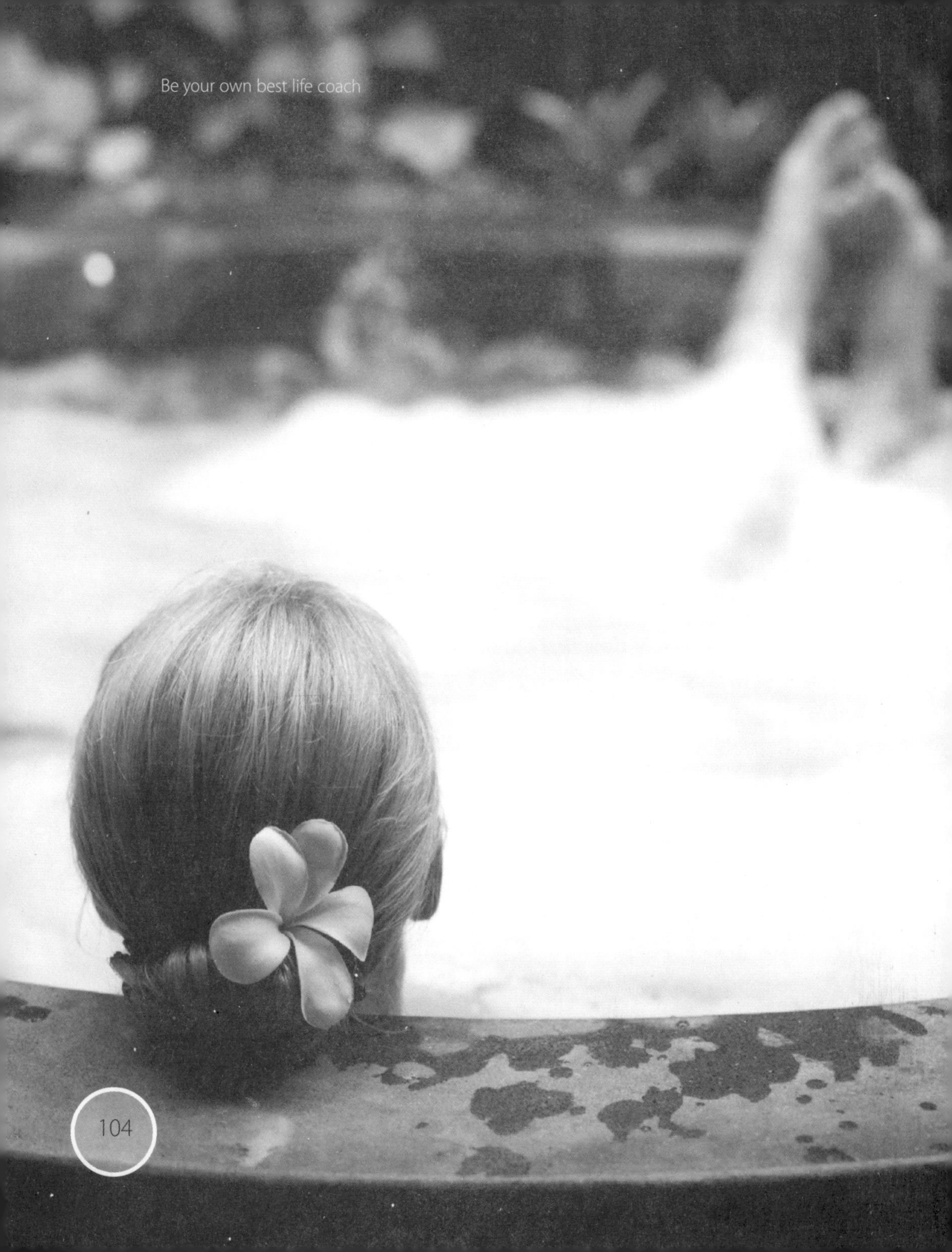

25. Let go of one thing

What's the one thing you could stop doing that would make a difference to your productivity? If you can work out the things to let go of, you'll get better at knowing what to focus on.

I've always been one of those people who loves having their fingers in several pies at the same time. But recently my list never seems to end. As soon as five things are completed there are ten other actions waiting to fill that space.

Smart coaches quickly realise that there are things that they do or systems they have in place that are no longer working and they set about getting rid of them. If you're anything like me I bet you've held on to your fair share of actions and habits that didn't give you the results you wanted.

When you start working with a coach it's very common to find that, rather than extending the list of things you want to do, your list of things to stop doing actually increases. The focus becomes prioritising what really matters. Individuals who work with coaches often find out that as they dive into what really matters, instead of taking on more projects and challenges they find themselves letting things go. They find themselves getting clear on what their priorities are.

Here's an idea for you...

The Slow Movement is rapidly spreading across the globe. Slow is the practice of one thing at a time. What about dedicating a day in your week to a slow activity? You could take off your watch for the duration of your activity; for example, take your time reading a good book curled up on the sofa, read a whole book to a small child, take a long uninterrupted bath, cook a slow soup or casserole, take a long slow walk through nature or around your neighbourhood, start a 1,000 piece jigsaw puzzle, eat dinner or lunch without any rush or – for those lucky ones – finish off your day with some slow love making (or do it in the middle of the day). Choose one idea and slowly enjoy it from start to finish.

Take a moment and just close your eyes for a few seconds. You can do this sitting at your computer or sitting on a bus. Think about all the activities you do in your day. As you scan the list try to identify which activities feel draining or give you that feeling of 'That's such a drag to do'. When that feeling or thought comes up notice it and write it down. If you stopped emailing for a day, would everything really go to pot? When I asked myself that question I realised I didn't want to spend my time responding to emails. I wanted to be writing articles, carrying out research and being a lot more creative. I was always busy but busy on the wrong things.

If you find a great idea that you want to achieve then, before you get to work on it, decide on the one thing you could stop doing that would give you more time and energy to focus on your goal.

In the middle of writing this book I was meant to start my training as a psychologist. I had been excited about this for months but as the time drew nearer I had this nagging doubt that I wouldn't be able to juggle the two projects at the same time. The feelings wouldn't go away and even though the course had been paid for, I cancelled. Immediately on cancelling I felt relieved but now I'm even more determined to take up my place later on in the year.

A little research threw up an interesting example of Marks & Spencer. In the 1950s Marks & Spencer went through Operation Simplification. The end result: dumping 26 million pieces of paperwork and selling off 1,000 filing cabinets. Radical, eh! Not bad when you think that we can use up to 22 minutes every day searching for paperwork.

Here are a couple of questions for you. What will be the one thing you'll stop doing and what goal or action will this allow you to focus on? Focusing on one thing at a time is the way successful people have always done things. You might be busy but you also might be sabotaging your success.

With so many options and choices nowadays, you will have to start saying no to some of the good things in order to accommodate the best things. Harold Taylor

How did it go?

Q. The thought of not multitasking frightens me to death. In my organisation the rule is that whatever it takes, we get the job done. Doing things one at a time may mean I miss deadlines and surely that can't be a good thing. What's the way out?

A. Many organisations thrive on producing good work but not great work. One of the benefits of focusing on one thing at a time is that you get to experience what it feels like to produce great work, because you're more likely to produce work of this calibre when you take on board this approach. This might be a good time to renegotiate deadlines and to let go of doing some things.

Q. Should I inform other people about the one thing I've stopped doing?

A. Don't feel pressurised to compromise your decision. People are far better at coping with change than they give themselves credit for. Be prepared for people to be intrigued by what you're doing. This may be the time to start sharing. Many organisations are actively changing workplace well-being practices and encouraging spending less time on emails and taking more time to rest.

26. Eliminate the things that drain you

One of the easiest ways to increase your energy and get great results is by the simple process of removing tolerations (things and people that drain your energy) from your life. So out with the old and in with the new.

In coaching the word toleration is generally applied to areas of your life where you're putting up with something without realising the cost to you in terms of energy, wasted time spent worrying and inconvenience.

Tolerations can include unfinished projects, incomplete household chores (things that either need fixing or replacing) and relationships that, when examined, leave you feeling drained. On closer examination you'll find that tolerations – whether physical, emotional or mental – drain your energy and distract you from the important tasks that will take you in the direction of success.

I know coaches who won't begin the real work with a client until they've had a go at clearing many of their tolerations. Why? Because when you start to tackle your tolerations you are creating more emotional, mental, creative and physical

Having problems deciding what to throw out? Choose an area of your clutter to work on, decide which category each item falls into and take the following action:

- I love this item and really need it – keep it
- I don't love it and really don't need this item any more – throw it
- I'm not sure how I feel about this item and I'm not sure that I really need it – add to maybe pile
- I definitely don't love this item but I do need this item – upgrade with a new replacement that you love

This system helps you be objective about what to let go and what to hold on to.

energy that you can then use to channel into your vision and goals. Leaving them unattended – even if you don't realise it – often means that the tolerations will eventually hold you back or certainly hold up your progress later on down the line. That's the thing about tolerations, it's so easy not to realise just how powerful they are in holding you back.

Coaching yourself on how to tackle your tolerations is easy. Take a good look at your life and make a list in key areas where you might be putting up with tolerations, for example home, relationships, work, health and well-being. Brainstorm as many items, from the small to the big, under each category. Once you have generated several items under each category, decide on where to start and get to work on clearing these tolerations as quickly as you can. When you're flushing out your tolerations leave no stone unturned. Most people find it easiest to start with their physical space. Take a look around. What needs clearing or fixing? Is it the filing cupboard in your office spilling over with paper? Or is it a drawer that's full of bits of paper you rarely refer to? What about the boot of your car, the cupboard under the stairs or the spare room that you can't move in?

Is there stuff that you could give away? Do you know about the Pareto Principle? Take a look through your wardrobe. How many of the items in your wardrobe do you actually wear? I bet it's a tiny proportion compared to what you actually own. According to the Pareto Principle you wear 20% of your wardrobe and the other 80% you don't wear. Choose five items right now and put them in a bag for the charity shop. Now that's one thing from your list handled.

What about tolerations in other parts of your life? What are you putting up with in your relationships? Whenever this question is posed in public workshops there's always one person who shouts out 'my husband' (sorry guys), much to the amusement of the others in the group who nervously laugh, knowing the comment is too close for comfort. Who are you putting up with? Which friends drain your energy and take up time? Maybe it's closer to home. What are you tolerating in your intimate relationship? Get to work on clearing these relationships too.

Keep working through your list over the next few weeks and months.
It's also a good idea to get into the habit of handling your tolerations on a regular basis. With your tolerations out of the way you'll attract better opportunities because you will have cleared space for what you want in your life. So get cracking.

It's not the tragedies that kill us, it's the messes. Dorothy Parker, American writer and poet

How did it go?

Q. I started off well with clearing my clutter but then I got overwhelmed. What shall I do?

A. When a task feels like too much it's always a signal to break the task down even smaller. It also sounds like you could do with a pair or more of helping hands. Get a friend who is good in their own lives with clearing clutter to give support. It might help if you give them permission to be ruthless.

Q. My list of unfinished actions extends to things I need to say in many of my relationships but some of these things happened a while back. Does it make any sense bringing these up now or should I just let it go?

A. I have mixed feelings on this and the reason for this is that I think it depends on the quality of the relationship you have with each person. If it is a relationship where you have regular contact with the person it may be fine to bring it up. However, if you've not had contact with the person in some time you might need to think more about how you raise the issue and the impact it will have on your relationship. Be prepared for a range of different responses. But it is absolutely the right thing for you to handle your incompletions. Well done for being willing to take this step.

27. Fight or flight? That is the question

We are a nation under stress. It is evident in the grind of the daily commute, the sandwiches eaten at speed at our desks and the TV dinners consumed with little or no connection to what's on the plate.

Stress has taken, and continues to take, its toll.

When my daughter was just six weeks old I started a new job. Being a single mother and anxious to prove myself, I threw myself into motherhood and my new job, determined to prove myself in both roles. Even though my job was challenging and rewarding I hadn't realised just how much energy I was giving out and how little I was putting back in. The body, being a wise vessel, waited until I was ready to leave for an overdue holiday to manifest a nasty ulcer on my right leg. It turns out that the ulcer was my body's way of telling me I was completely out of balance.

The body's normal stress response is fight or flight, different reactions to perceived potential threats. The problem comes when we don't factor in space for the body to rest after an onset of stress. Stress is further increased by emotional triggers such as worrying, visualising a difficult conversation or frustration with your job or relationship. Stress accumulates and lack of rest weakens the immune system, which leads to illness.

Here's an idea for you...

Here are some tips on how to short-circuit your stress:

- Sit quietly in your car for ten minutes after arriving home instead of leaping out immediately after you've switched off the engine
- Once a week take a packed lunch to work and at lunchtime head out for your local park, museum or local attraction on your own
- Once a fortnight get into work an hour earlier and enjoy quiet space before the office buzz kicks in
- Once a week hit the pillow at around 9 p.m. and get up at 5 a.m. – just think about what you could do with the extra two hours
- Once a week have an evening indoors minus the television or DVDs. Instead catch up on a good book, listen to music, do some gardening or repot some plants
- In the next ten minutes take a nap

But there's also another way to look at stress, and that's your perception of it. Have you ever thought about why some people handle stress better than others? Think about high-pressure jobs like surgeons and pilots. Even though their bodies go through the physical responses of stress they've been trained to respond and know that they can control seemingly stressful situations.

What's your normal response to managing stress? Do you reach for a glass of wine, another helping of food, or perhaps you escape in front of the television? Whatever method you choose along these lines, what you're actually doing is inviting the stress in rather than pushing it away. These and other unhealthy habits only serve to increase stress, not control or reduce it.

Imagine what you would do differently if you took control of managing your stress. Instead of taking time out in front of the television, could you take time out in nature, take a short stroll or enjoy a hot bath? Do you really need to reach for another plateful of carbohydrates or will a plate of fruit be more nourishing for your body? You'll need to take charge because the hormones cortisol and adrenalin that ignite the fight or flight responses are the same hormones that signal to the brain the need to replenish your energy that's been used up. The presence of cortisol makes you want to refuel quickly with cakes, biscuits or pizza. Direct your brain to the right food source.

Stress is a norm of modern-day life but building in time for rest and relaxation will lessen the impact stress makes on your body. When my daughter was young I used to head for a steam and sauna session every Friday afternoon on my own. It made a difference to how I felt. Write a list of rest and relaxation activities to do when feeling stressed. It really does help to plan what you will do beforehand as it's so easy to slip back into those old stress-inducing habits.

Our stress isn't a result of the event but of the view we take of it. If the event is seen as negative then we set ourselves up to experience stress.

Ellen J. Langer, Professor of Psychology, Harvard University

How did it go?

Q. I generally find I get a lot more done when I'm under stress. But recently I had a check-up and it appears I have high blood pressure. Do you have any suggestions for how I can lower my stress but at the same time maintain my performance?

A. Best to always back up with proper medical advice but in the meantime here are some thoughts. Some stress is good. But you need to replace what's been taken out and used up. Eat fruit and vegetables like grapefruits, bananas and tomatoes that are high in potassium, magnesium and fibre and whole grain for that extra dose of fibre. If you're not exercising, start now. Brisk walking at least three times a week for 30 minutes or more helps to lower blood pressure and improves cholesterol levels. If you want to plan routes and check the distance you walk use the brilliant website www.walkit.com, which covers London, Birmingham, Newcastle and Edinburgh.

Q. At the moment I am drinking two or three glasses of red wine every night as a way of coping with stress at work. Am I drinking too much and what can I do to reduce my drinking?

A. Advice on recommended safe drinking limits vary. General guidelines are twenty-one units per week for men and fourteen for women. So, going by these guidelines, yes, you are drinking too much. On a practical note you drink more because your body becomes dehydrated, so drink a glass of water between every glass of wine. Are there other things you can do that will take the focus off drinking? What about joining an evening class or engaging in an activity with your children? Find a healthier substitute for your stress relief.

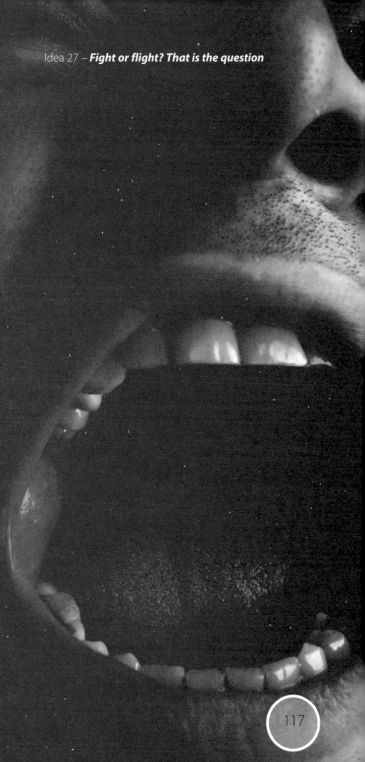

28. The worry code

Do you find yourself worrying and obsessing over everyday concerns? Not sleeping at night because of all that's on your mind?

Help is at hand. There are productive ways to worry. Here's how.

By now you're well aware that as you work on changing your life you need as much mental and physical energy to support you with your changes. No matter who we are and how in control we believe ourselves to be, we all worry from time to time. So what can you do to turn your worrying into something positive?

Focus on productive worry
The key to worrying is knowing the difference between productive worry and unproductive worry. I know it's really obvious. But I bet you've fooled yourself into thinking that all the worrying you've been doing will actually help make the situation better. The answer doesn't lie in worrying until you're less anxious either. Well, think again. To counteract your worry you actually need to be very proactive. Start off by asking yourself whether your worrying is a problem that you can do something about right now (or very soon). Asking this question very early on can stop you from ruminating and fabricating all sorts of stories that tend to be based on 'what if' scenarios which generally generate unproductive worry and rarely lead to getting anything solved.

Take action

Once you decide that something can be done then it's time to swing into action. Let's say you're having problems with your housing. What is a realistic action that you could take? Could you write a letter or make a phone call? Don't worry about having to get the whole thing under control. You won't be able to answer all the questions right now about your housing so there is no need to focus on the unanswerable questions. Keep focused on taking tiny or small actions. The kinds of worry that feel niggling are often a result of things that we've just never got round to sorting out, like unanswered emails (don't we all know that one), leaking taps and unfinished work. Avoidance only intensifies your worrying. So do what you can as soon as you can.

> **Here's an idea for you...**
> Carry out a little experiment to see how accurate your worries are. Think ahead and make a list of all the things you worry might happen in the next fortnight. Two weeks later, gather up your earlier musings. Take a look and record what did actually happen. What percentage of your worries actually came about?

Ruminate on a way out

Worrying often leads to catastrophising (imagining worst-possible scenarios). I know it's a long word but isn't it infuriating when you catch yourself saying out loud the worst possible things that could happen? Even worse when no sooner have you found a solution than out pops another catastrophising statement, one to replace the one that's just been resolved. We're all guilty of it in some shape or form. But there is good news. Thanks to the work of cognitive therapy (cognitive therapists help you change the way you think and what you believe), there's a way to challenge this. Substitute your negative thoughts with positive ones. Every time a worrying thought presents itself try imagining the best possible outcomes. Instead of a negative story spin yourself a positive one. We remember stories so frame them positively and they'll work more in your favour. Taking the time to ruminate in this positive way will actually reduce the time that you worry.

Embrace uncertainty

Sometimes the pressure is on and it just feels like there's not a lot you can do. When we're faced with uncertainty it can feel much easier to push the fear of the unknown away and fixate ourselves on what we can have control of. I'm sure you know those moments when you can't control the traffic hold-up that's going to make you late for an important meeting. You're likely to misuse your time worrying about the traffic rather than surrendering to the moment. This is an ideal moment to practise the Buddhist technique of mindful detachment. Take a deep breath and sit back and gently observe everything around you. Acting in this way focuses you on being in the present moment.

When it comes to worrying, take action where action can be taken. But to keep on top of taking the action, keep yourself on track with practising these techniques as often as you can.

Don't worry about perfection. You'll never find it. Salvador Dali, artist

How did it go?

Q. Worrying just seems to be part of my nature. My mum was the same. She still managed to accomplish a lot in her life. Isn't worry just the way some people are?

A. Yes, I can see what you're saying. I grew up with a mother who was constantly worrying. But as I watched and reflected on the quality of life it gave her I decided that I really needed to curb some of my own worrying. Worrying is learnt behaviour and what was learnt can be unlearnt. What do you worry most about? Isolate your worry concerns and apply some of the above techniques. The exercises above are simple and not hard to do. I think that you'll find over time that you can and will teach yourself to worry less.

Q. I get very emotional when I worry. Is there something I can do to not be so emotional?

A. This is actually a good sign. It's important to feel your emotions and not push them away. Keeping an emotions diary may work here. Write down the things you're worried about, what happened, what led up to it and the emotions you may be feeling. It might help to shift your perspective, seeing your feelings written down. Is there a pattern emerging? When you look at your list you may find that things are not as bad as you think.

29. Going that extra mile

Excellence is all about bringing your best self to the table.

Whether or not you're acknowledged, it's about your personal commitment to doing your best and going beyond what's expected of you, it's about going that extra mile without thinking about the reward or the prize.

When would you go that extra mile? There's an old story based on the Roman law that a soldier could ask a citizen to carry his pack for a mile. Being a law, the citizen had to do it. As the story goes, one day a soldier saw a citizen and said, 'Would you please carry my pack?' The citizen not only carried the soldier's pack one mile, but carried it an extra mile as well. The impressed soldier asked, 'Why did you go that extra mile?' The citizen replied, 'The first mile was for the state, and the second mile was for you.'

A few years back a German couple opened a small café around the corner from where I lived. Unassuming from the outside, all that changed once inside the doors. The cups they served tea and German coffee in were of the best quality, as were the plates meals were served on. They served sumptuous and appetising Italian food cooked with love. The café only seated about thirty people, so finding a table wasn't always easy. Word about Terra Firma spread around the area and within months it was a thriving café/restaurant.

A year later they opened for dinner in the evening. This must have been the time I started piling on the weight for I'd head there under any excuse just to delight in their food. I so loved that place that I hired the restaurant for my 40th birthday celebration. There was uproar in the community when the couple moved on. Customers were genuinely sad. Terra Firma was a living example of what it was like to run a business that had excellence at its core.

At secondary school, history was my favourite subject. Whilst all my classmates sniggered about my history teacher's habit of spitting when she spoke, I was too engrossed in the period we were studying to even care. Every Friday we'd be set a project to complete over the weekend. The project needed to have an attractive front cover, designed by us, pages of content and a conclusion. I would rush out of school and head straight for the library, eager to get to work. All weekend I would pore over the project. By the time Sunday evening came I would be drooling over pages of neatly written italic handwriting complemented with illustrations and brightly coloured drawings. I would treat each project in much the same way as monks treated ancient manuscripts. I'll never forget the feeling of pride I experienced when I handed in my project on a Monday morning.

The next three to four days would be spent in eager anticipation. We would get our results in class on the following Friday. I loved the A+ for effort, the A+ for

Here's an idea for you...

One way of getting close to excellence is to steep yourself in the practice of doing something badly. Choose an activity that you'll be willing to have a go at and allow yourself to do it as badly as you can. When we allow ourselves to do something badly we take our focus away from worrying about how things turn out. We discover new things and there might just be a possibility that because you are not worried about how things turn out you actually do something really well.

achievement. Back then this was all about my thirteen-year-old self going that extra mile. That was one of my first initiations into excellence. No matter how poorly I did in other subjects, my achievement in history always brought a smile to my face. And gave me a lot of joy.

Excellence can be instilled in the smallest of tasks to the largest of projects. Excellence in one area can easily be transferred into another. Consider the following:

- Could you start by buying a more expensive brand of envelopes?
- Could you pay more attention to the time and effort you make in presenting your evening meals?
- Will you add something to a meeting that surprises everyone, like a small box of chocolates to share as a way of saying thank you?

Excellence is what you do to raise something to the best standard that you possibly can. Everyone has some area in their lives where they can demonstrate excellence. Your job is to find it and then, by extending the same approach, coach yourself to excellence in other areas of your life.

Any activity that makes you happy is certainly inside your arsenal of excellence.

Barbara Sher, career counsellor

How did it go?

Q. How does a commitment to excellence differ from being a perfectionist?

A. Great question, to which I have a simple answer. There are two simple ways to distinguish between the two. Perfectionists tend to procrastinate and deliberate over details, whilst those committed to excellence are committed to getting the job done and enjoying the rewards.

Q. I have faced a lot of backbiting and underhand comments from family and work colleagues because of my ability to do things really well. It just seems to be something I have a natural ability to do. This has meant that at times I've held myself back. I don't really want to go down that road as I enjoy my work so much. Can you help?

A. This is a very common challenge. I come across a lot of brilliant people who are working to half their capacity because of wanting to blend in with the crowd. But I want you to agree that this stops now. Have you thought about either looking for a new job or thought about where you might be able to use your talents much more successfully in the organisation? A sideways move may be just as lucrative. There are companies crying out for personnel like you. Your skills and strengths are in demand, so work this to your advantage.

30. The good, the bad and the ugly

All defining moments in our lives are variations on all three of the above. Your take on those moments will impact on the way the movies of your own life end.

What defining moments can you remember? Start with your childhood and work forwards through your life.

I kept an article that I clipped out of *Marie Claire* back in 1999. It told the story of the Haenyo women, which literally means sea women, some as old as 80 and others as young as 37 who regularly dive off the coast of Cheju Island, 60 miles south of the Korean mainland, holding their breath under water for up to ten minutes. They have kept this 800-year-old tradition going and such is their passion and commitment that one woman described going diving the day before she gave birth to her son.

You may not have held your breath beneath freezing waters but your defining moments will have felt pretty much the same. I'll never forget the gorge I climbed in South Wales. I was one of the group leaders on an outward-bound course for graduates in the mountains of South Wales. I hadn't quite geared myself up to just what this meant. But when I found myself faced with accompanying our group up an 800-foot gorge my immediate thought was, no way am I going to do this.

The defining moment came to me when we were making our final ascent to the top of the gorge. There I was climbing fearlessly up a steep hill and I realised in that moment, as I was grappling to find the next rock to grab hold of, just how strong and confident I had felt – a confidence that had steadily increased throughout the day.

What about you? Your defining moment may not have been a physical act. It may be coming through a difficult time, or a time when you found yourself on a huge learning curve or suffered a deep loss. These moments, both challenging and happy, can be looked upon as defining moments.

One of the things I want you to do is to give time to acknowledging your defining moments, because we have a tendency to overlook our personal moments of power in favour of valuing and acknowledging the power moments of others. Make a list of your ten most powerful moments in your notebook.

Here's an idea for you...

Practise this exercise to strengthen your ability to make decisions confidently. Emotionally, the solar plexus – a large cluster of nerves tucked behind the stomach slightly below the diaphragm – affects breathing and posture. It's here that you first notice feelings of fear, anxiety and intuition. These gut feelings often play a role in decision-making. When breath flows freely through this area, you'll feel more confident, grounded and secure. Lie down with your palms facing up and close your eyes. Picture a yellow flower, its petals fully open, and place the flower in the region of your solar plexus. Take several deep breaths and as you inhale and exhale imagine the flower floating up with each inhalation and down with each exhalation, riding a slow, gentle wave. Focus on your breath and the flower for two to five minutes. After five minutes slowly open your eyes and come back into the room.

A workshop exercise I have used for years is entitled 'A time in my life when I was powerful'. The idea is for each person in the group to share a moment when they stepped into their own power. Like the time you stood up to the bully in the school playground, or the time your speech at your best friend's wedding made the whole room cry. This exercise has never failed to demonstrate the enormous potential and power located within each individual.

Your power moments are at the core of your truest self, which some psychologists refer to as the essential self. Make a list of powerful moments in your life and then pull out your skills, qualities and abilities that were expressed by you in the moment. Look for the patterns in your power spots. These might include things like:

- I was quick thinking
- I was resourceful
- I displayed grit and determination

If you had these qualities back then, you could still have them now. So use them; don't let your natural skills and strengths lie there wasting. We don't tap into our defining moments enough.

Insufficient appreciation and savouring of the good events in your past, and over emphasis of the bad ones are the two culprits that undermine serenity, contentment and satisfaction. Martin Seligman, psychologist and writer

How did it go?

Q. *I find this concept difficult. I mean there really is nothing that stands out from my own life that I could put into the category of a defining moment. I tend to just get on with things. Any suggestions?*

A. Divide your life up into seven-year periods. For each period imagine you're now in your late seventies and talking to your grandchildren. They're eager to hear stories about you and your life. What episodes or incidents will you tell them about? What memorable moments will you retell? What moments when you made a stand will you share with them to nurture their courage? Whichever events and experiences you choose will be fine.

Q. *Many of my defining moments are tinged with sadness and regret. I'd rather not go back and get in touch with them. What should I do?*

A. Returning to look at your past experiences doesn't need to be traumatic. Imagine yourself as an observer on your past, looking at it from a distance. Tell yourself what you see. What can be learned? It's really the learning and the wisdom that you need to extract.

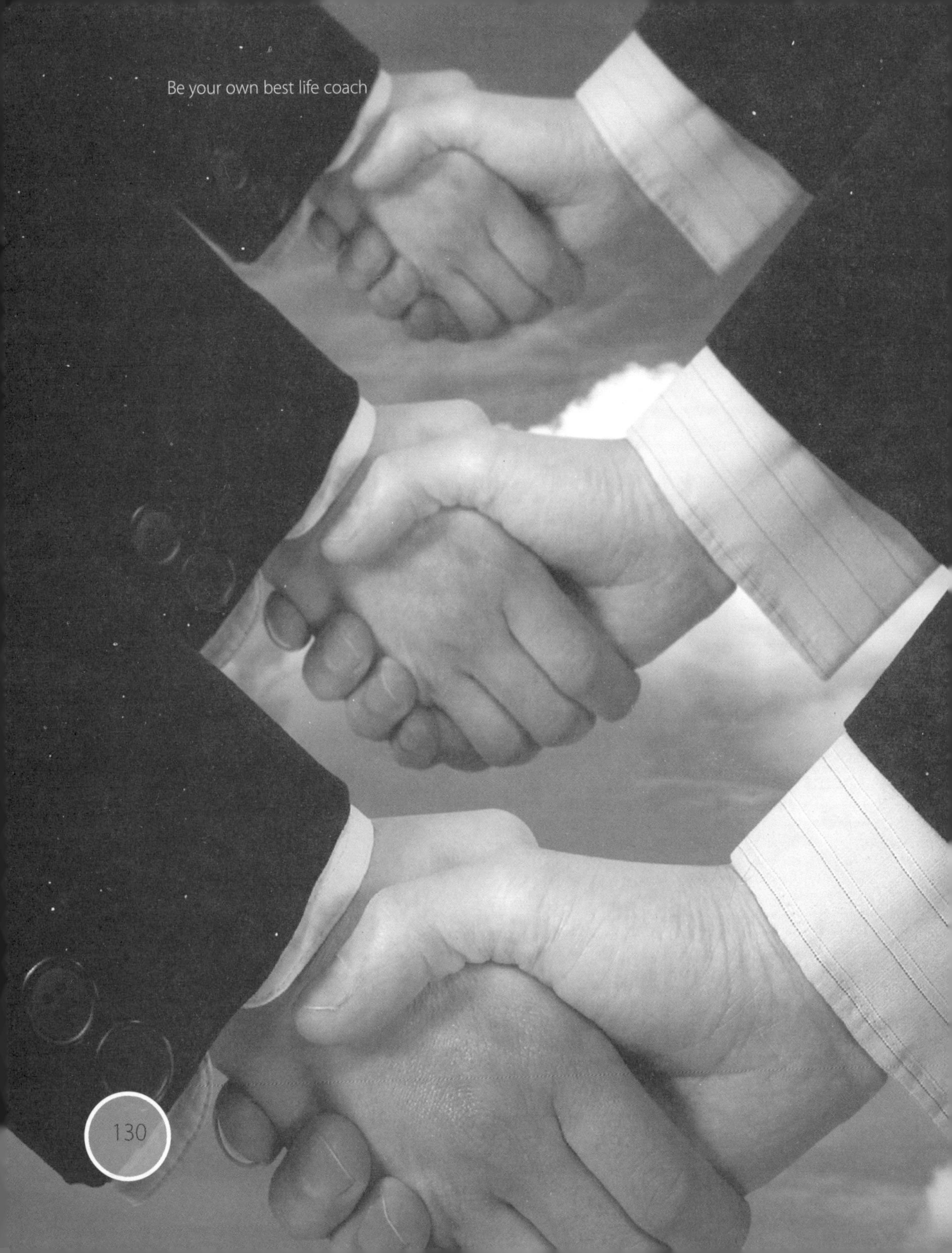

31. Get life confident

Whether you believe it or not, the more action you take in your life, the more confidence you'll develop. Action begets confidence and not the other way round.

Over the years my views on confidence have radically changed. I used to believe that once I'd mastered this confidence thing the world was my oyster. But the confidence I know about and witness when working with clients is far from being a permanent feature.

Every time you feel a dip in confidence I want you to remind yourself about something one of my coaches told me that I'll never forget: 'Confidence doesn't always come before the act but will often make its presence felt after.' Many people achieve great things in their lives without much confidence in sight. And even then, confidence is not guaranteed for the next act or venture.

When I started running I wasn't confident at all. My first run was not a pretty sight. I chugged around my local park looking pretty pathetic, to be honest. On the last stretch of the run, which was unfortunately up a hill (why hadn't I worked this out

Here's an idea for you...

As soon as you wake up take a deep breath right where you are and repeat the following sentences several times: 'In all of the world there is no one exactly quite like me. Everything that comes out of me is authentically me because I alone chose it.' Spend the next five minutes repeating all the wonderful things that make you who you are. For example, I am loving. I am wise. I am intelligent. I am beautiful. I am resourceful. I am funny. I am thoughtful. Use language that works for you. The opening lines for this practice come from the beautiful poem I Am Me, written in 1975 by family therapist Virginia Satir (see www.avanta.com).

before I'd started?), an elderly woman walking her dog chose the moment to tell me, 'You might as well give up, love.' I couldn't believe it. There I was, not much confidence to begin with and now here was some stranger trying to shatter the tiny smattering of confidence I had left. What I hadn't fully connected to in that moment was that I didn't need confidence to complete my run. That came after. I needed persistence, staying power and determination. But most of all, in order to build and strengthen the possibility of growing your confidence you'll need to take action. Whenever you feel low or lacking in confidence, take action. Remember, confidence is the by-product of action. Once you're taking action, gather your evidence.

Here's a short test. Can you recall any instances of positive feedback you received in the last two weeks? I'll be surprised if you can recall them all. What about feedback from a month ago, three months ago? Yes, it's surprising how little of the positive feedback we receive that we convert to memory. That's why I want you to get into the habit of writing down any feedback you receive. Now how about creating a compliments folder, a personal record where you'll keep your written feedback in one place? Take your list as far back as you want and include everything, from the smallest compliments to your biggest successes. Find yourself a brand new notebook or file. A folder with twenty or more plastic wallets is ideal. Every time someone appreciates or validates you in writing print it off and archive it in your folder. When someone gives you feedback over the phone, take the initiative and write the feedback down. Take it one step further and post copies of your feedback in places in your home where you'll see them often. Really, I mean it. I want you to see and be reminded of your feedback every day. You've had years listening to negative reviews so now it's time to put on a different tape. It really will boost your confidence.

I am always doing things I can't do, in order that I may learn how to do it. Pablo Picasso, artist

How did it go?

Q. My partner has just left me for my best friend and my confidence has plummeted. What can I do to feel better and improve my confidence at the same time?

A. I'm really sorry to hear that. It's OK to be mad for a bit – it's normal and healthy. But don't be mad for too long because I want you to try something. What I want to suggest to you is that whether you feel like it or not you get yourself back out there again on the social scene. Not necessarily to bag a new partner – even though of course that might happen – but so you can get evidence that you've still got what it takes. Elsewhere in this book we've talked about faking it until you make it and the fact that other people see us differently to how we see ourselves. This stuff works. Getting back out there you'll quickly be reminded just how attractive you are. You'll take your mind off your break-up and you'll be distracted while having fun.

Q. I recently completed training as a psychologist. It took almost three years and a lot of hard work and now I've been told that I am not coming across as confident at interviews. What can I do about this?

A. What did you most enjoy about your psychology training? When you talk to others about that aspect of the training are you confident? Do you know what makes you feel confident? Is it the way you sound? The body language you give off or your passion? Make a note of all the things that contribute to your coming across and feeling confident. Choose one of those qualities and create a signal that will connect you to it. You could call up the feeling or make a small movement to connect you to it. Use your trigger to move you to a place of feeling confident.

32. Creativity unlimited

We're all born creative whether we tap into our creativity or not.

Getting coached on how to be creative may seem pretty dumb. But it's amazing how many people are cut off from a real source of personal fulfilment that can improve how you feel about yourself and the work that you do.

We're all creative, not just some of us

Whatever job you do, or whether you're a stay-at-home parent, everyone has the ability to be creative. Being creative at home or at work is a skill that we can all employ, but many of us fail to fully put it into practice. Many people write off their creativity in favour of making the mistake of believing that creativity is some mystical gift reserved for talented artists. OK so we won't all be a Damien Hirst, making millions from his high-end art, or become best-selling authors like J.K. Rowling.

Opportunities to express yourself creatively are everywhere but we often neglect to nurture our creativity in favour of demanding tasks and items on our daily to do lists that we deem more urgent and important. Being creative is as much about the care you put into folding the laundry, or the attention you give to placing a bunch of flowers in a vase, to the way you present an everyday meal that resembles a work of art.

Here's an idea for you...

You don't have to wait to have time or money to be creative. There are plenty of ways to be naturally creative in your everyday activities. As part of wedding gifts to their guests my two friends made bouquets of flowers placed in empty shiny baked bean tins. What could you do to add more creativity to your everyday tasks and activities? What about adding creative flair to personal correspondence? I regularly decorate personal letters (a rare treat) to friends and family with butterfly stickers. Think about three activities in your week where you could add your personal creative touch to everyday actions and activities.

Many people get stuck when it comes to deciding what they want to do creatively. Try this to help you get unstuck. Imagine you are being interviewed on radio or television on the topic of 'Exploring your personal creativity'. What would your response be to the following questions?

- What activities did you enjoy doing as a child?
- If you had more time in your week, what creative outings would you take yourself on?
- What creative activities would you try if you could?

So what things did you enjoy doing as a child? Let's say you loved drawing as a child. What's to stop you carrying around a small sketchbook with you? You can sketch on your way to work or while waiting in reception at the doctor's or the dentist's. Designer Paul Smith carries around both camera and notebook as he never knows what inspiration he will come across in his day-to-day activities.

Here's a man that many would describe as being at the top of his profession yet he is still dedicated to a very simple and humble creative practice of notebook and camera. He gives his mind creative licence to be on alert throughout the day.

Studies have shown that owning and expressing your creativity lowers stress levels and increases your sense of well-being. Recent research has revealed that where employees actively express their creativity employee productivity improves and the benefits to the organisation are significantly increased. Other studies have shown that by stretching your creative muscles it enhances your problem-solving skills and improves the quality of your communication with others.

As coach, your job is to keep a constant check on just how connected you are to your creativity, even in small ways. Identify activities that will allow you to be more creative as you go about your day.

I can always be distracted by my need for love but eventually I will get horny for my creativity. Gildna Radner, actress and dancer

How did it go?

Q. I find it difficult to even keep up with a creative practice for even a short amount of time. Can you offer me any suggestions?

A. Hey, let yourself off the hook. I bet you are being creative throughout your week but you just don't know it. Look for examples of your creativity in less obvious places than traditional artistic pursuits. Instead ask yourself this: What outfit have I worn in the last week that I felt really good in? Got one? Well, there's an example of your creativity at work. Can't think of an outfit? Well, how about making an event of your journey to work this week? Take a camera and take photos of buildings and people, just for the fun of it. Download them on to your computer, print them off, make a collage or create a storyboard. Pinpoint where you are being creative in everyday activities – then keep it simple and make it fun.

Q. There's a course I really want to do that gets me all excited about its creative potential. But when I presented it to my boss at work I was told they wouldn't pay for it because it wasn't relevant to my job. How can I convince them otherwise?

A. Now here's the deal. Do you really want to do this course or not? Or is this just a way of you giving yourself an excuse to just not go ahead? If you really, really want to do this course, why not simply decide to fund the course yourself? Yes, really. There's no way you won't win. You'll get to enjoy a course you really want to take. You'll learn new skills. Taking the initiative will demonstrate your leadership qualities to your current boss and a future employer. Once you commit it's amazing what manner of opportunities will rise to support your decision to go for it. So put in that application and go for it.

33. Out your creative monsters

Was your natural creativity and spontaneity interrupted at some point early on in your life by critical individuals who failed to see the value and gold in your creative expression?

It's time to take charge and slay the creative monsters from your past.

When I was a child I really did love to sing. OK I didn't always know the words, and still don't, but singing was something I just enjoyed doing. My love for singing was put to rest quickly by the arrival of Mr Muzzard, the head of music at my primary school. He spent his entire teaching time eliminating any love or enjoyment of music in every child he came into contact with. In his case that meant almost the entire school. Years later I still remember his caustic remarks and how he would reduce children to tears. Mr Muzzard was what you call a creativity monster. He loved putting out the creative lights of others; perhaps in very much the same way his creative lights had been dimmed in the past. Who were your creativity monsters? Who shamed and humiliated you creatively? Name and shame five people right now.

Now let's have some fun with a serious issue. That's another thing you'll learn as a coach. Humour is a good technique when your material is in danger of getting too deep.

Here's an idea for you...

Sometimes feedback from a critic can be illuminating. The secret lies in keeping control of the conversation and directing them towards the questions you want answered. Think specific, not general. Ask questions like: 'What techniques do you suggest using to improve the plot in my novel?' or 'How can I improve the quality of my overall design and look?' as opposed to, 'Did you like it?' or 'Was it OK?' which are signs for a critic to attack. If unwanted feedback slips into the response simply separate the specific from the personal and extract the bits that you need.

Let's name your creativity monsters in much the same way that characters have nicknames in stories. Let's call Mr Muzzard the Music Monster. OK. Now what's the worst punishment we can give to the Music Monster? Help me out here. All right, he may have been dealing with his own creative shame but nonetheless I'm punishing my Music Monster to a lifetime of listening to a choir of children singing out of tune. That would have been torture for Mr Muzzard. From now on his job will be to tell his choir of children all day long how beautiful they sound. Now that feels good and it made me laugh. Now it's your turn. What fate will you assign your creative monsters? Name them all and then assign each to their fate.

Even as adults the part of us that creates has a childlike quality and it's this part of the self that was criticised, attacked or wounded for its creative endeavours and, as a result, this part of the self can be prone to vulnerability. When it comes to coaching yourself around your creativity, proceed with care. So allow your creativity a little space for tenderness.

Now I hope you are feeling a lot more hopeful. I didn't want to become a singer at all but singing made me feel good. When we're allowed to express our creativity freely it just makes us feel good. Now move on to completing the next exercise. With no emphasis on product or performance what would you have a go at just for the heck of it?

Grab your notebook or journal and write: 'If I didn't care about results or performance I would try …' Finish the sentence and then repeat several more times.

Pick one item from the list and make a commitment to give it a try. No pressure. Just get to it when you're ready and in your own time.

The opposite of a creative monster is a creative champion. One way of making peace with our creative monsters is to become a champion to someone else. Is there someone you could become a creative champion to? Is there a young person who could do with a lift? Could you let someone know how much you are inspired by their creativity? Giving others what we so needed ourselves can be both healing and transforming.

Creativity is allowing yourself to make mistakes. Art is knowing which ones to keep.

Scott Adams, creator of the *Dilbert* comic strip

How did it go?

Q. I'm having a hard time ignoring my internal critic. Is there anything I can do to unleash its grip?

A. Change the way you relate to your inner critic by being creative on a regular basis, because regular attendance to your work fools the critic into thinking you're not doing anything that important. It is more likely to pounce when we've left work to the last minute and try to get it done in one last swoop. I'm sure you're beginning to see the irony of it all. So keep plugging away. Soon you'll notice them less and find yourself doing the work no matter what.

Q. My daughter is a brilliant artist. I really try to encourage her but she's constantly putting herself down. I don't want to make too big a deal of it but do you have any tips when it comes to nurturing a child's creativity?

A. First thing I want you to do if you haven't done it already is to take one of your daughter's drawings and frame it. There's something quite spectacular that happens when a painting, sketch or any hand-created image is suddenly framed. Get your daughter involved. Then together walk around your home and get her to choose the spot where she would like it displayed. You'll be amazed at the change in how she feels. But be warned: a trip to IKEA may be called for. Once in a frame, always in a frame.

34. Go for a walk

Feeling blocked? Need some inspiration? Why not use the time-honoured natural remedy and take yourself for a walk?

Walking is as old as mankind itself. Every tradition and culture has a long history of walking. From the African and Aboriginal ceremonial walkabouts and Christian and Muslim pilgrimages to Native American Indian vision quests, walking has always been in our blood.

British writer Charles Dickens was one notable lover of a long walk. Dickens, however, loved to take his walks late at night when he would literally bump into strange and unsavoury individuals whose personalities were transformed into characters in many of his novels. Not that I'm recommending you do the same. Taking walks will be safer in daylight and will also afford you the opportunity to burn calories.

OK, I know what you're thinking: 'I just don't have the time.' Well I've seen all kinds of people with hectic schedules and responsibilities rise above the challenge of time by starting off small – a five-minute walk around the block, three or four times a week. Soon the five minutes extends into fifteen. Before you know it not only are you looking forward to your walk but eventually you'll start walking for longer.

Once you're out there with the air and wind it's important to set your focus. Why not walk with an agenda. No, that doesn't mean bringing along your mobile phone or your iPod. In fact, if you can, leave mobiles, iPods and any other digital equipment behind. For now assume them as banned (all right, you can sneak in a digital camera). If you're worried about forgetting ideas, walk with a pencil (not a pen as they tend to stop writing when held the wrong way up) and a small packet of Post-it Notes or an index card. Set the agenda by walking with a question in mind. Hold your questions gently in your thoughts and get on with enjoying your walk. Do the same with something that you're worrying about. Instead of ruminating, walk. Most people find that they return from walking with problems and questions solved.

If you live in London, Birmingham, Edinburgh or Newcastle, check out a great website, www.walkit.com. Type in your journey and it will give you times for different levels of walks, map out your route and tell you the distance you've travelled. They're hard at work on adding new cities so don't worry if yours is not there yet – it

Here's an idea for you...

When you hit a creative block or feel disconnected from your creativity this is a sign to practise what the Buddhists refer to as Loving Kindness. Think of it as your creative comfort food. Perhaps in your early years no one came to your rescue. When we were children we may not have had anyone to soothe our wounds or take care of our damaged egos so now, as the adult, it is your job to do the taking care of. Items on my list of small acts of kindness and tenderness include:

1 A hot bath with oils or sea salts
2 Spending an hour or more reading for pleasure
3 Solo trips to the cinema, museums, galleries, book readings
4 Buying organic foods for dinner
5 Spending a Saturday afternoon watching DVDs
6 Lunch at the weekend with friends

Now make a list of your own kindness treats and apply when you feel creatively blocked.

145

might be soon. Planning your walk with 'walkit' is a great way of feeling good about the distance you've covered each day.

You'll quickly see how by walking you'll in fact save yourself time because problems get solved, ideas get generated, you gain more energy and, for those worried about your figures, calories are burnt off. How's that for a great problem solver? If that's not enough, the physical benefits include significant reduction in the risks of stroke and heart disease, breast cancer and type 2 diabetes. Walking also helps to maintain flexibility and strong bones and muscles and promotes cell growth. So come on, what are you waiting for? Get walking.

Solvitur ambulando — It is solved by walking.

St Augustine of Hippo, fourth-century theologian

How did it go?

Q. *I find walking boring. Nothing much seems to happen to me either during or after. Shall I persevere for a little while longer or should I jack it in?*

A. Well something is happening. You're already receiving some of the physical benefits and that in itself is worth every walk. Have you thought about increasing the length of time of your walk? Some people actually need a longer time to unwind. This might be the case for you. At least try getting a long walk in once a week and see if that makes any difference at all. Also try varying your routes.

Q. *I'm blocked creatively. I remember as a child writing plays and acting out scenes for friends and family. Now I'm a mum with two small kids and I see my life slipping away. I do have time on my hands but I just can't seem to get excited about anything. Can you suggest anything else that will get my creative juices flowing again?*

A. In addition to the walking I suggest you get hold of the book *The Artist's Way* by Julia Cameron. She is one of my favourite writers on creativity and writing. Fifteen years ago this book pulled me out of bed and a deep depression. It's a 12-week course that includes keeping a journal and writing in longhand three pages of thoughts first thing in the morning. In addition, the course includes walking and taking yourself on artistic dates. It is well structured and inspiring enough to get you moving. Try buddying up with a friend who is in the same boat. And one last suggestion, why not pen a play for your children and, when they're old enough, act it out?

35. Try a little tenderness

We're much better at taking care of others than we are of ourselves. But the most important person to start taking care of is you.

Enjoy ways to make you feel good. Self-care demands much more than the occasional beauty treatment or physical bout of exercise.

Self-care is about eating nourishing foods, taking care of your spiritual and emotional well-being, spending quality time with friends and family, taking yourself away on retreat. No waiting until you've run yourself into the ground or you're running on empty. Your self-care needs to be ongoing and topped up on a regular basis with self-care treats.

It's so easy when you're busy to forget about your self-care rituals. So why not keep notes on the things that nourish you? Create a self-care list of ten things that nourish you. Refer to the list when you feel depleted or drained. You're more likely to make better choices about your self-care at that moment than reaching for a handful of crisps or a glass of wine.

One way of getting to the root of your self-care needs is to dig out your guilty pleasures. One of the best ways to build your reserves is through guilty pleasures. Guilty pleasures are the things you know that if you did more often would make you feel better, but you don't. 'I really could do with a break from the kids but would that make me look bad as a parent?' 'I wish I could have an evening off from the family but I only feel justified to do that if I'm working.' Most of the time you know exactly what you wish you could do to give yourself some *me* time – you just feel guilty about doing it. And herein lies the challenge. The things you feel guilty about doing are often the things that are good for you. So go on, make a list of all the things you feel bad about wanting to do. Go on. No one has to see your list except you. You'll squeeze loads of the juice out of the word guilt just by noting down your guilty pleasures.

Want some regular pampering, then why not turn an everyday routine into a luxury indulgence? There may not be time for a visit to the spa or the funds to book yourself in for a full beauty treatment but that's no reason to put your self-care on hold. A normal bath can be upgraded to a four-star treatment by paying that little bit more for good-quality bath products; adding a few fresh flowers and

> **Here's an idea for you...**
>
> For more bathtime bliss go green in the bathroom by recycling everyday ingredients raided from your kitchen cupboards and fridge that won't cost the earth. One or two tablespoons of ground ginger added to your bath stimulates circulation. Add seven drops of your favourite essential oil and two tablespoons of organic honey into a jug or large bowl of semi-skimmed or organic milk. Warm up in the microwave for three minutes and add it to the bath. For smooth skin grate the rinds of four to six oranges, lemons and limes into your bath for a zestful skin tonic.

a tray of candles to give the room that extra special feeling; as you step out of the bath pat yourself dry with an extra large and fluffy bath sheet that has been warmed on a radiator.

Give yourself the spa treatment before you step into the shower. Polish up dull-looking skin by rubbing on a body scrub, starting with the soles of your feet and working your way upwards using circular movements.

For a do-it-at-home facial fill the bathroom sink with warm water and add three drops of lavender essential oil. Men may prefer to try three drops of peppermint or eucalyptus essential oils. Soak a warm flannel in the fragrant water then head for the bedroom, lie down, cover your face with the cloth for ten minutes and inhale the aroma.

What's the one self-care habit you've neglected? Work on reinstating it over the next seven days.

Perhaps we are all scrooges when it comes to self-nurturing, because if we were kind to ourselves, our creativity might begin to blossom like a plant moving toward the light.
Sarah Banbreathnach, author

How did it go?

Q. I find it really satisfying to take care of others. Am I doing something wrong?

A. Achieving balance is important. It might not feel like it right now but sooner or later you'll begin to feel depleted. So in order to keep on giving and getting the satisfaction that you do it's important that you find ways of treating yourself in the same or similar way. What do you do so generously for others when you take care of them? Could you do the same for yourself? What could you do for yourself regularly that would feel special? Have fun with coming up with imaginative ways to creatively take care of you.

Q. Isn't it selfish to put yourself first?

A. Putting yourself first is central to your success. Your self-care will ensure that you have the energy and the focus to get on with your goals and do the things that will help you achieve your success. Not only that but your self-care will also ensure that you will feel good about you, which gives you energy that can be channelled into your relationships and connections with others. Think of it as being self-full not selfish. It's selfish to deprive ourselves. That's the most selfish thing you can do.

36. Passion power

What lights your fire and what puts it out? Let's find out what you need to do to keep your passions alive.

One of the quickest and most revealing ways to get in touch with your passion is to discover what moves you. By this I mean the little things as well as the big things.

You're going to get smart at coaxing out your passions and reminding yourself of the value and importance of doing the things that bring you joy.

My first memory of really being moved was in junior high. It was a custom for the teacher to read aloud a story to the class at the end of each day. On this particular occasion, at the end of our Friday afternoon reading of *The Famous Five* by Enid Blyton I felt that I couldn't survive the weekend without knowing what was going to happen next. I rushed home and then out to my local library and I borrowed a copy of the book and devoured it over the weekend. This marked the beginning of my passion for books.

What experiences and events have moved you in your life? What activities made you feel joyful or at least gave you a feeling of contentment? Think back as far as childhood. Many of your most potent memories will reside there. At this stage there's no need to be attached to what those memories meant. Just allow yourself to get back in touch with them. You'll know these memories because they'll feel warm and familiar. Something about the experience will have stayed with you. Note what you remember in your notebook.

It's one thing to retrieve your memories of your passions and joy and another thing to commit yourself to living them. Just think about it. If you were to act on the many things on your list what would your life look and feel like? Yes, you bet, you would be able to put this book down because you'd probably be living a great life. Part of the reason you will need to coach yourself in this area with a lot of tenderness and care is because we often resist and deny ourselves the things that will change our lives for the better. Right now go within and ask yourself whether you are afraid that your passion will ask more of you than you are willing to give. Ask yourself the question that you don't want to be asked. I know it's weird but it seems to be human nature to do the opposite of what we really want.

Here's an idea for you...

Don't think passion, do passion. Gather your list of joys and passions and plan a passion fest weekend around your items. Try to enjoy at least one passion from your list a day, but the more you give it a go, the better. So if one of your passions was baking cakes, get out the baking bowl and flour. If you loved drawing, buy yourself a sketch pad and draw. Remember this is not about product, this is about pleasure. When that smile comes on your face or there's a tingle in the centre of your stomach, you'll know you've struck gold. You can extend your passion weekends to include your partner or a group of friends.

It's true that sometimes our passions take more than we think we have to give. But thankfully those are not the only passions we have to rely on. Begin by tucking some of those other passions and joys into as many spaces in your life as you can. I still get a tingle in my stomach and a rush of adrenalin whenever I walk into a library or a bookshop or attend an author book reading, really I do. One way I keep on top of these passions is to make sure I can fit them into and around my schedule. When I'm away for work I always make a point of finding out where the local library is. I always have a book on me, well almost always.

Bringing your passions into your everyday life is infectious. Your joys big and small will spill out into every area of your life. When you feel stuck, overwhelmed or depressed, turn to a small joy or engage with one of your passions. A life on purpose is a life full of passion.

Passion roots in the oddest places.

Katherine Russell Rich, breast cancer survivor

How did it go?

Q. My challenge is the opposite. I have too many passions. I want to do it all and can't seem to get moving on any. Please help.

A. I definitely know the feeling. People like you and I are what coach and career counsellor Barbara Sher calls Scanners. That's why I want you to get hold of a copy of her great book, *What do I do when I want to do everything?* But there's one problem here. Wanting to do everything means that it's highly likely you won't be doing any of the things you claim you're so passionately interested in. Funny that. By holding on to this approach you're holding back on getting what you want. I suggest you put this book down right now. Write down your top three passions and commit to just engaging with one – yes, only one – for the next six months.

Q. What's the difference between an interest and a passion?

A. An interest doesn't hold and command your attention and attendance in the same way that a passion does. You can be interested in something but only take notice of it when it is put right in front of you. A passion is much more consuming. You'll find that with a passion you're more likely to take a risk or be willing to make sacrifices. You are more willing and compelled to be the seeker and to seek out the passion and make it a part of your life and what you do.

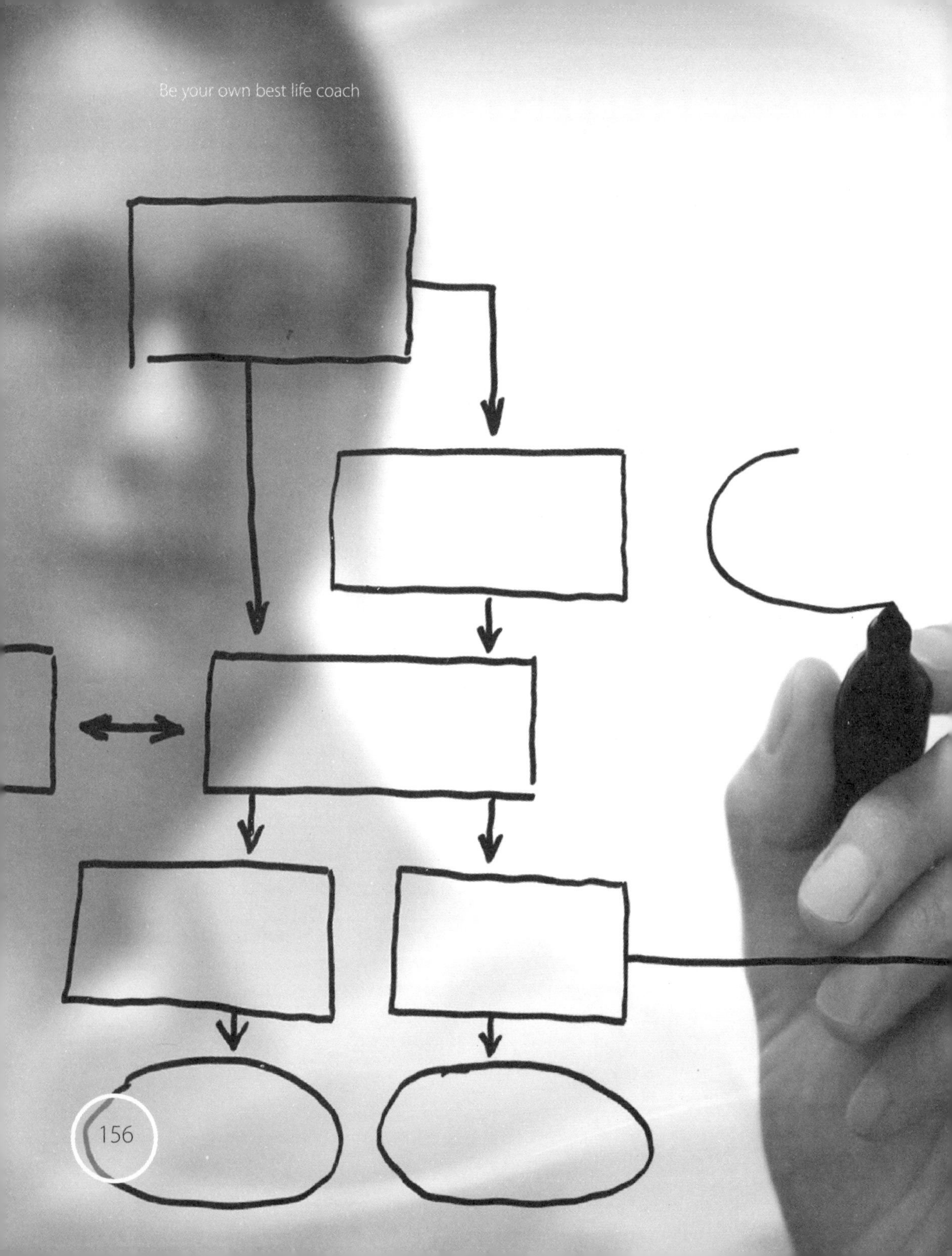

37. Hit the sweet spot

No, not the latest Masters and Johnson sex therapy tip but a novel way of finding out what it is you really want to do with your life. Get creative and have fun designing and fulfilling your own life purpose.

Feeling under pressure to know just what your Life Mission is? Don't worry; help is at hand.

According to Jim Collins, an entrepreneurial professor that I found via Pamela Slim's excellent blog www.escapefromcubiclenation.com (great for those wishing to leave the corporate world and set up in business), find your sweet spot and you'll find your Life Mission.

The sweet spot Collins refers to can be found in your answers to three important questions and finding the place where the findings from your responses interlock and meet.

Draw three large interlocking circles on a blank page. In the first circle write about your deep interests or passions, subjects you're energised and engaged by; hobbies, amateur interests, obsessions or causes you're fired up about.
In the second circle write about the things that you enjoy doing that you know people will pay you to do – marketable skills and abilities that you've developed over your working life.

Here's an idea for you...

Take one of the activities you love doing and brainstorm as many different ways you could get paid doing this one thing. Brainstorms work great with a group or on your own. Break training traditions and hijack brainstorms from training rooms and take them on to the streets. They'll go down a storm on nights out with your mates, with crazy and often great ideas being suggested. Share your brainstorm with strangers who won't care about censoring ideas. Run the same brainstorm for several days or even weeks, soliciting ideas wherever you go.

In the third circle write about the activities you enjoy doing that find you at your best, the things you're excellent at doing – the things only you do uniquely well. In other words, the activities you'd do just because of how much you get out of doing them.

Where these circles interlock is where you'll feel fully engaged, motivated, fulfilled and joyful about your life and your work. This is the centre of your Life Mission or calling.

One morning I sat at my desk savouring the moment, enjoying the quietness that covered our home as everyone slept. Even though the words weren't fully formed in my head I rushed to my journal and started to write.

What I wrote about in between the opening and closing lines took me by surprise. You know that way sometimes our processes and growth run ahead of us and we're just catching up. My words were an acknowledgement of my own sweet spot. I wrote about the gratitude I felt in that moment, knowing that I was in a place in my life where I was being paid to research, write and read to my heart's content about topics and subjects I was deeply interested in and passionate about. I was having fun being creative and developing and shaping my thinking. In that moment I realised how important it is to savour moments like this even when the smallest thing in our lives, our work or our relationships moves us. You may not be in your ideal job, have found your soul mate or be living in that perfect home but each moment savoured in this way makes the journey towards your sweet spot even sweeter. In introspection I realised in one divine moment I had found where my passions, loves and desire to be of service meet. The sweet spot is your template to do the same.

Now it's your turn. By taking the plunge and answering the questions even if you're not exactly where you want to be, your responses will steer you in the right direction. And you'll also have a blueprint for what it will look like once you get there.

Vocation is where your deep gladness meets the world's great hunger, that's where you're going to find your calling.

Frederick Buchener, Presbyterian PCUSA Minister

How did it go?

Q. So many of my friends have taken the plunge and left the corporate world for the world of self-employment. I love my job and I love the people I work with. But my friends make me feel like I'm afraid of change. What can I do to make myself feel better about my decision to stay?

A. Congratulations to you for making a stand for what you believe in. This might also be a good time to check yourself and consider a few questions. Are you keeping up with current changes in your field? Is it time to learn a new skill, take on more responsibility or think about stepping up your game? What do you really love about your job? How is this organisation a great match for your values? Change is a constant. Without it, none of us grows. Answering these questions will strengthen your confidence in your decision.

Q. What if getting a job in the areas I identified in my sweet spot are hard to come by?

A. Welcome to the real world. There are plenty of ways in which you can engage your interests while working towards a more established career in that sector. Why not start a blog around that area? Become a fan of bloggers who work in that area. What about volunteering or finding a mentor who works in the sector? Do what you can that will keep you connected and think outside of the box to keep those connections flowing. The more experience, knowledge and expertise you gain, the stronger the position you will be in at a later stage. Be excited by the possibilities and opportunities you could create.

38. Will the real Mr, Ms, Miss or Mrs … please stand up?

What does it take to be the real you? Bringing together the parts that you love, loathe and hide are the beginnings of the new authentic you.

I would love to tell you that I've been a good person all my life but I haven't. I've been good in some parts and not so great at all in others.

I, like you, have had my fair share of life challenges, certainly not anything much different from anything you too may have gone through: abuse, domestic violence, depression, low self-esteem, been lousy with money, losing myself in relationships, lied and then lied again some more, neglecting friendships, been challenged with addictions, gossiped about everything and everybody and managed to alienate myself from most of my family. Doesn't paint a great picture, does it? But then again it doesn't paint the whole picture either. That's because if I continued with the list I could equally add that I've grown loads from all my experiences and mistakes, learnt even more by repeating the same mistakes again, helped hundreds of people over the years in a variety of ways, been compassionate and kind, been a loyal support to friends, given birth to a

Here's an idea for you...

Start a collection of self-portraits. A self-shot photograph taken through a mirror or a reflective surface is more likely to show your real face rather than the expected approved look and smile. Try taking a photo of yourself as soon as you get up in the morning. No need to put on a smiley face if you don't want to. How about taking a series of self-portraits for seven days? With digital cameras you can experiment and delete (well, maybe not so much on the deletion) to your heart's content. Try capturing your self-portraits at different times of the day. For more on self-portraits go to www.mirrorproject.com.

beautiful daughter, written two books and numerous articles, stayed with a partner who I love despite our many challenges and picked myself up off the ground too many times to mention. I write this list and the one before not to brag or boast but because if I'm asking you to step up and show your authentic self then I wanted to reach out and take the first step with you. What would a list outlining the aspects of your whole self (the shadow and the light) look like?

Wearing a mask may have been one way of coping with this split self. But the joining of the two selves really begins when the presence and contribution of both the shadow and the light is both honoured and acknowledged as equally valuable contributors to your growth. The shadow gets given such a hard time and that's why, at this point, it's always good to bring in a bit of humour. Some of the best breakthroughs I've had have been those moments when defences have been down and I've been able to laugh at my own flaws and foibles. Sharing specific examples of your shadow self with a group of people always seems to lessen the shadow's energy.

One way of doing this is to reveal a secret you've been holding on to to one or more people. I will never forget a leadership course I did years ago where one by one we each shared a secret that we were ashamed of in front of the group of around thirty people. It was one of the most liberating moments I've experienced. Now I'm not suggesting you gather all your colleagues at work and let it all out. But what about thinking about the different ways in which revealing your secret could be done? You could send a letter, make a phone call or initiate a conversation. What about telling your secret through your work creatively in a painting or in a range of writing forms? Sharing your secret weakens its power to shame you. It's legitimate now to share yourself on your blog. I read an amazing apology by a blogger to someone she had offended with a comment she made about them in a national newspaper. In it she took full responsibility but told the story eloquently and honestly shared what she had learnt. It took my breath away.

And the day came when the risk to remain tight in a bud was more painful than the risk it took to blossom. Anaïs Nin, diarist

How did it go?

Q. I'm not ready to tell other people. Is there a step before?

A. Actually there is. How about writing a letter that you don't send? Or, alternatively, write about your secret in your notebook. Some people have enlisted the help of a therapist and role played the secret and worked it through that way. After this your next step could be to rehearse telling your secret. This will help relieve anxiety before you're ready to share your secret with someone else.

Q. I'm out about my sexuality outside of work but finding it hard to come out at work. Do you have any suggestions for coming out at work?

A. There's no right or wrong way of doing this. Coming out is an individual choice and some of it will be trial and error. However, you may be very surprised by the response and support you receive. Some people may already be aware of your situation and feel as relieved as you when it's all out in the open. Others may want to be supportive but may find that your personal choice conflicts with their own personal values. I suggest you keep an open mind and be willing to take things a step at a time. Get up to speed on your company's policies on equalities and make sure you continue to draw on the support from both outside and inside your work. Good luck.

39. Know your strengths

Want to get ahead? Then focus on your strengths. A good starting place is to ask yourself: 'What am I naturally good at that other people find hard to do?'

If you were stopped on the street and asked to list as many of your strengths and weaknesses as quickly as possible, which list do you think would be the longest? We all know the answer to that one.

The majority of us would probably struggle with our strengths but be able to reel off a long list for our weaknesses. We're notoriously good on puffing up our weaknesses and dumbing down our strengths.

We're all born with a portfolio of strengths that develop and grow as we do. Some of these strengths emerge naturally and are often qualities and talents we were born with. Charlotte Church's natural strength is obvious – singing. The strengths we are born with often don't feel hard to exercise. We develop other strengths as a product of the environment we were raised in and from experiences we pick up along the way. Consider these your acquired strengths.

Here's an idea for you...

Ever thought of having more than one type of CV to hand? Have a go at devising a Courage CV. A Courage CV highlights key roles, life challenges, places in your life where you stepped out of your comfort zone, achievements and transformations and things we forget to mention that traditional CVs often leave off. Here's a template for writing your own courage CV. Make a list of ten events from your life that required both large and small acts of courage on your behalf. Whilst this type of CV may not be every organisation's cup of tea, it might be a breath of fresh air in some. Having a range of CVs to hand allows you to highlight your strengths in a range of creative forms. Take a peek at Sofia's own CV on her webpage www.turnupthecourage.com for creative ways of laying out your Courage CV on the page.

But what about the things you're good at doing but don't enjoy? Do these count as strengths? I'm a good cook but I don't advertise this as one of my strengths. Because on a day-to-day basis cooking is not something I really enjoy. I do it because it has to be done. Not quite a natural talent but a strength I learnt growing up. It used to irritate me being called into the kitchen by my mum when I wanted to be outside playing like my brothers. But it meant I developed a skill in cooking.

If someone asked you outright to outline your strengths, could you say them out loud without mumbling and stuttering? Most of us would probably rush through them in embarrassment, just wanting to get the whole thing over and done with. OK you might brace yourself to appear confident in an interview or assessment centre but most of us would rather do a bungee jump than have to proclaim our strengths out loud.

But there is a danger in not acknowledging your strengths. You're more likely to live a life that's based on your weaknesses and find yourself constantly trying to catch up with yourself, rather than taking a more assertive approach and focusing your life on the things you enjoy doing and are good at.

Next step is to get clear on what your strengths are. But a little pep talk before we continue. In order to get ahead in this game you're going to have to agree not to generalise. That means naming things. So, saying you're good with dogs will not be considered a strength. It will only be validated when you specify exactly what breed of dog you are particularly good at working with. The same goes for the statement 'I'm good at communicating'. Again, this says nothing about the communication skills that you have. Your job is to flesh out the detail that might be obvious to you but not to others. 'I'm good at teaching people how to dance', or 'I help and support people who are trying to work through conflicts in a relationship'. Again get specific. No detail, no strengths. At the same time, don't make the mistake of only looking in the obvious places for your strengths. Look to your losses for strengths that may have emerged from there. You'll notice as you start being specific and detailed that this ensures that the strength is defined as something that you can actually do.

It takes a stranger thirty seconds to sum you up. Practise saying your strengths aloud in thirty-second sound bites in front of the mirror.

You will grow the most in your areas of your greatest strengths. Marcus Buckingham, consultant

How did it go?

Q. How do you know the difference between a strength and something that you're good at but it's not really what you want to do?

A. The difference between the two is this. One may fill you with fear but you just can't help being drawn to it. Writing feels like that for me. And the other one you could be really competent at but it always leaves you feeling drained and unfulfilled in some way. You'll need to be aware though that this doesn't mean that engaging in your strengths will always leave you feeling high. But the difference will be in the quality of knowing you've just engaged in some rewarding hard work and feeling energetically depleted and drained with little satisfaction from the task.

Q. What if your weakness is holding up a part of your business?

A. Find someone else whose strength lies exactly slap bang in the centre of your weakness. It will be easy and effortless for them to handle the issue that is blocking you. Release yourself from the struggle. Get it handled by someone else. Why do we give ourselves such a hard time trying to do everything ourselves?

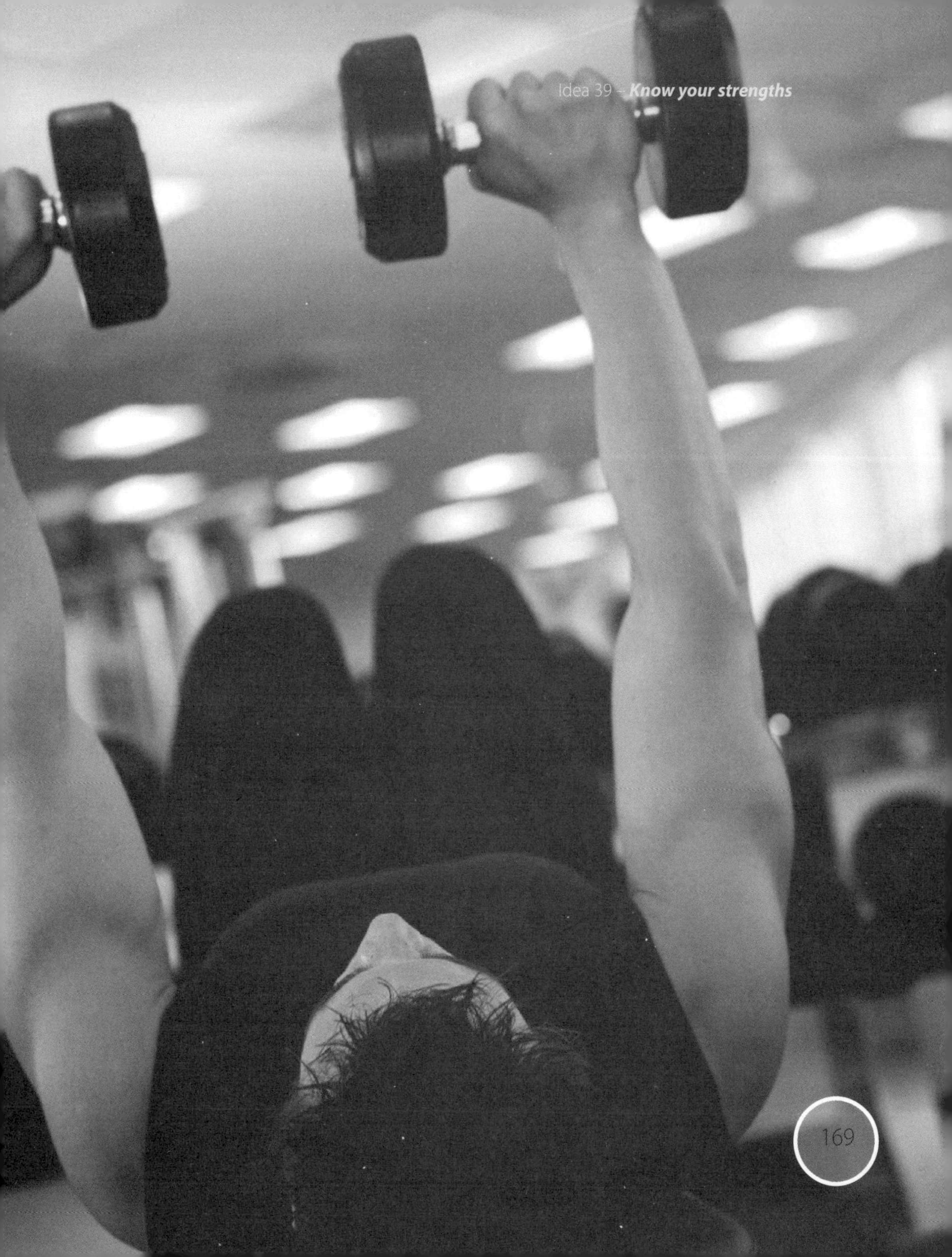

40. Emotions unplugged

Ever wondered what it really takes to get a handle on your emotions?

How about knowing what it takes to balance your emotions with more appropriate responses?

Here are some options available to you:

Option 1

Keep a journal where you freely express your emotions by writing down how you feel and any worries or concerns you may have. Use the page as your dumping ground. It's OK to say here exactly what you want to say to someone but you know that saying it face to face wouldn't be a good move. Don't hold back. This way you'll have an outlet for your emotions so they won't have to find other ways of getting expressed.

Option 2

It's possible to think without feeling the intensity of your feelings and emotions. This is something cognitive behavioural therapists do when working with victims of post-traumatic stress. Think about a particularly stressful or difficult period in your own life. Observe yourself as you're thinking. Are you feeling any of the emotions that you felt around the time of having the experience? You may feel a little something but I bet it is nothing like what you felt back then.

Practise putting your emotions on hold, until you're ready to deal with them.

Option 3

It's good to get into the habit of distinguishing what emotions you do want to connect with and the ones that you don't. Often emotions with opposite impacts sit very close together. For example, passion and rage and anxiety and enthusiasm are very close neighbours. Both sets of emotions draw on similar forms of energy, but again with different impacts.

Option 4

It's easy to get caught out thinking that emotions have to be responded to on the spot. You could decide to have or feel the emotion when you're in a place of safety or in the privacy of your own thoughts. Your boss criticises your work in front of one of your colleagues. A hasty response may lead to an unwanted result. However, you could choose to tell yourself, 'I don't have to have this feeling right now. I'll have it later when I'm at home.'

Option 5

Don't rush a response, instead step back and take time out. I wish I had taken time out years ago when a friend approached me, wanting to give me some feedback. My emotions spiralled out of control as I brought to mind many times

> **Here's an idea for you...**
>
> What are three emotional responses you would like some help with? Describe each example in a sentence or two on a separate page in your notebook. Switch to writing with your non-dominant hand and slowly – there's no rush – draft a list of facts, alternative responses and options under each of the emotional challenges. Don't worry about whether your writing is legible or not. The slowness and deliberateness of writing with your non-dominant hand will give you an insight into the speed in which the neocortex works. It may also uncover ideas and thoughts you may not have considered before.

before in my life when I had been criticised. Even though I trusted my friend and valued our friendship I gave my power away to my past in that moment. So rather than hearing her out I defended myself and promptly told her where to stick her feedback. I don't recommend this as a way to keep friendships.

Option 6

Get used to confronting your emotions and seeking information that will discount a negative emotion. Let's say you feel you were embarrassed in your team meeting at work. You feel upset and angry and are about to give it to the person who you see as the main attacker of your presentation. Another way to manage this is to pause. Ask yourself, 'What have I missed?'. Did you miss the fact that two of your colleagues spoke up on your behalf? Have you really given yourself time to think about a more useful way of responding to this? The more time you give yourself to search for facts and evidence, the more you take back your control.

At the end of the day, despite the wide range of emotions and feelings available to us at any given moment, remember that many of your feelings are not for action.

A man's mind stretched by a new experience can never go back to his old dimensions.

Oliver Wendell-Holmes Junior, American poet, physician and essayist

How did it go?

Q. I was expelled from school before taking my final exams. I started working at 17 and have been working for the last ten years. But not having any qualifications is really getting to me. I'd love to go back and study. What can I do to break through my fear?

A. Well-known chef and author Delia Smith left school at 16 without any O-levels. Is there an area you're really interested in exploring? Make enquiries about what's available. Mature students are well known for gaining significantly better grades and for having a much richer experience both in terms of enjoyment of learning and scoring higher in relationships and social skills. It might also help to talk to a mature student about their experiences. Contact your local university or college and ask to be put in touch with one of their mature students and interview them about their experience. You've got loads going in your favour. Go for it.

Q. I find it hard to control my anger when members of the public are rude to me. It's come up a couple of times in my appraisals. Any tips on how to manage my anger?

A. Try out the 'Stoplight approach' used in school Anger Management classes.

- Red light – stop, calm down (take two or three slow deep breaths) before you speak or act.
- Yellow light – think of a range of things you should or could do (not just your first impulse). It might help to write these down either before, during or after the incident.
- Green light – pick the best one and try it out. If that doesn't help try another one.

41. The sixth sense

Magical powers, a sixth sense or just common sense?

Can you know when a vibe is right or just a red herring?

Within minutes of being introduced I took an instant dislike to the woman who would at a later date become a very close friend and buddy. As I write we've been good friends for over twelve years. It seems that as powerful as some of our intuitive hunches are, they're not always right. One reason for this lies in the fact that the emotional pathways that run from the eye to the brain's emotional centres often bypass the cortex and we react emotionally before we have the time to process the information fully. Once the cortex – that's the thinking brain to you and me – has time to process the information, we start to make different interpretations, such as 'Oh, I do like you after all.' Now come on. I know I'm not the only person who does that.

At the same time, don't be fooled. As much as your intuition can sometimes be wrong, it can also be gloriously accurate. To prove it to yourself, in the next ten minutes see how many examples you can come up with of your intuitive hunches or vibes being proven right whether you acted on them or not. Is there a common thread to any of your examples? This is a question you might want to keep on asking yourself because you are best equipped to decipher your personal history and relationship with your intuitive intelligence to know what works. When I posed the same question to myself and looked through my own examples one of the common themes I noticed was that when I acted on my intuition from the quiet place inside me, the outcomes were positive. Another theme that emerged was how acting on what seemed at the time as ridiculous urges have a pattern of producing surprisingly good results even when those results were years in coming. Here's an example of what I mean.

Several years ago I met a friend for lunch in our local park. It was a hot day so we took shade under a small tree. As we prepared to leave I was drawn to a small plaque that gave a short description of the tree. For some reason – and at the time I had no real evidence as to why I should – I felt a strong urge to write the information down. Following this episode I became more and more interested in learning and reading about trees. This led to me researching and reading up about the tree I had sat under that day, which was in fact an elder tree. Fast forward a couple of years. I am sat in my local library, putting the finishing touches to my first book. Taking a break I distract myself by browsing through the books on the shelf behind me. One book catches my eye, a book on surnames. I look up the meaning of my surname, 'Holder', not expecting to find anything of interest and am greeted with the

> ### Here's an idea for you...
>
> This is a version of a game I learnt at a BBQ. One person is chosen to be the guesser. Have everyone sit in a large circle or close together. Give the instructions that everyone has to think of two things that are true about them and one thing that is a lie. Choose one person to be the guesser. The guesser then has to work out who's telling the truth and who isn't. If you guess that someone is lying then that person becomes the guesser and the game continues. Play the game until the last person is left in.

following inscription: 'The name Holder was the name given to people who lived near to elder trees.'

Your intuition won't always be accurate but sometimes it will lead you to the most astonishing discoveries. The more you practise, the clearer you'll become in distinguishing between those moments when you're gripped with the 'I don't know why I'm doing this but I'm going to do it anyway' feeling and other times when you'll be confident that it's time to sit back and wait a while.

Not everything that can be counted counts, and not everything that counts can be counted. Sign in Albert Einstein's office

How did it go?

Q. I'm male and in my job I often regret not saying things and not acting on my hunches and watching other people getting the recognition because I held back. Is there a way I can feel more confident about taking the initiative and sharing my ideas?

A. One strong element of harnessing your intuition is the ability to follow through. This often requires a disciplined approach in testing out your ideas through sharing them and engaging in discussion and feedback. Some of your ideas will be welcomed and some rejected. The more you practise sharing your ideas, the better and more confident you will become until it feels like second nature.

Q. I'm extremely intuitive. I give accurate readings to my friends but now I 'm getting a weird reputation and my friends avoid telling me things about what's going on in their lives. I'm beginning to feel misunderstood and isolated. What do you suggest I do?

A. There's a thriving community of people just like you out there called clairvoyants, psychics or intuitives. These are people who have undergone professional training and have chosen to honour their talent of seeing into the future or having strong intuitive receptors. Many have trained for years under the tutelage of experienced practitioners so they can harness these skills in the best possible way. It may be time for you to start spreading your wings (not a phrase to share with your friends). I'm sure that once you find the right community your balance will be restored.

42. Reinvent your life

Does it feel like time to change direction? Would you like to set yourself new challenges and start afresh? If you could start all over again, what might your first step be?

Using these four easy steps you'll learn how to coach yourself through the journey of making the move from where you are to where you want to be.

Making this choice is about stepping out big and not hiding your light under a bushel. You're letting the world know that these are the changes you've made and this is what the new you stands for.

I know you're probably thinking 'This sounds great but, personally, where on earth do I start?' Sorry to disappoint you but, like all things, it's going to take some hard work on your part, but it will pay off. Use the four Rs model as a guide to getting from start to finish.

The four Rs of reinvention
- Research: Do your research. You can always tell the person who has invested time in doing this. What they have to offer has a freshness and a crispness to it. Have you gone out and interviewed three people working in the field you're

interested in moving into? Have you done any shadowing? On one of my radio appearances I came across a company (www.vocationsvocations) that offers two to three days (yes, you do have to pay for this experience) shadowing someone already established in the field you're interested in moving into. Now how cool is that?

- Release: Make your move as clean and as smooth as possible. That means paying attention to the ways in which you leave and say goodbye. Make sure you've tied up all loose ends and had closure. One year I gave away all my books on a certain subject area. Another year I gave away outfits that did not fit in with my new look. Don't just stick to objects. Ask the don't-want-to-ask question: 'What beliefs do I need to release?' Doing this work first will make the reinvention a smoother transition.

- Reaffirm: You may be letting go old skills and areas of knowledge, values and beliefs. But which of these qualities will you be bringing with you? No need to throw out the baby with the bath water. When I started speaking more on radio I realised that a lot of the skills I used in working with people still applied. Make a point of reaffirming the strengths and skills, values and beliefs (positive ones I hope) that you'll still be using. Making a conscious effort to identify and acknowledge your existing skills and resources is another important step as you make the transition.

Here's an idea for you...

Draft an email or letter to someone working in the field or industry you'd love to learn more about. Maybe you're interested in working in magazines or would like to pursue a passion in photography. Outline who you are, what prompted your request and what you would like to explore and find out about in three days of shadowing them. Keep it short and concise. Even if a huge reinvention is not part of your plan right now, who might you consider sending your letter or email to? Now you have your draft, either send it or save it for a rainy day.

● Reinvent: How will you stand out from the crowd? Take a look at who's out there leading in the field or profession you wish to move into. What can you learn from them? This is not about being competitive. This is about appreciating the successes of those who are leading and learning from them. What services, products and skills will it be important for you to embrace? Think also about the value you bring. Make your mark not just with your business or career but also in your appearance.

Madonna is the modern-day example of reinvention from her female archetypes of the whore and the virgin to mother and wife and respectable lady of the English manor. Whatever our thoughts on her radical reinvention, take heart in your own. Consider your reinvention not as a dismissal of your past but as the next step, a natural evolvement and alignment of your skills, strengths and talents. Reinvention is the modern-day career move.

I am going through the layers and reinventing myself. I am on a journey, an adventure that's constantly changing shape. Madonna

How did it go?

Q. I have gone through a complete cycle of reinvention but my best friend and I are drifting apart. What can I do?

A. This is very common when people make changes and part of the reason why we resist making changes. We're afraid of what other people might think. Your friend's distance may be triggered by her own fears and insecurities which could include grief about losing the friend she thought she knew. Try having a heart to heart and talk about how her behaviour is making you feel. Remind her about what you value and appreciate about her. If this doesn't change things then it may be time to accept that your relationship has changed and it is time to move on.

Q. I've been on maternity leave for eighteen months and have decided not to return to my old job in retail. Instead I want to retrain as a chef but the thought of having to start over again is paralysing. Can you help me unlock my paralysis and head for my dream career?

A. Good news first. Focus on your retail skills that you'll be able to successfully transfer into catering. Were you good at sorting out problems or understanding complex information about a product? Many of these skills will still be of value in your new career. Now for the bad news: being willing to reinvent yourself and your career is very likely to involve having to make the sacrifice of being willing to start at the bottom and work your way up. Focus on how much you'll learn and how much more experienced and qualified you'll be.

43. It's all about your contribution

Focus more on giving yourself wholeheartedly through your work or your actions rather than on what you can get.

Focusing on your contribution will take your life to a whole new level.

The mounting pressure to be successful, to hit unrealistic targets and to stay on top of ridiculous deadlines creates enormous stress to survive in a competitive driven, prove-yourself culture that sees many of us losing sight of who we are and the real value of our contribution to others.

Your contribution is one of the most valuable assets you own

There are easier ways to genuinely contribute what we know, what we are skilful at and what we are passionate about outside of pressurised environments in the work place. Have you ever noticed how anxiety and worry about your performance lessens when you get caught up in the excitement and enthusiasm of what you are doing?

Here's an idea for you...

Volunteering is a great way to practise making a contribution to others. Do you know what opportunities exist locally that could benefit from your time, skills and knowledge? Volunteering offers the chance to share without the pressure to perform and worry about what others might think. Take a look at www.timeback.org.uk for innovative volunteering opportunities. Offer as little or as much time as you like. Abandon the attachment to praise and accolade in favour of the real value of connecting with others wholeheartedly in your valuable role as a volunteer.

Getting to this place requires tapping into a level of contribution that can be greatly enhanced when you focus on how you make a difference to others without attachment or expectations. This could be anything from assisting a frail, elderly woman to cross the road to helping out a stranger who is clearly in distress. This level of contribution takes the focus off the 'I' and refocuses it on the 'We'. It is not uncommon for people to feel significantly better and confident about themselves and their abilities when they tune into contributing to others without expecting anything in return. Such acts of kindness and generosity that are not based on rewards can see you arriving at your desk feeling energised and motivated or engaging in conversations with a partner or family members less distracted and with more openness and empathy.

Putting your best self forward

When I was at school there was a bus conductor (a job sadly now extinct) who looked like he had been plucked straight from the stage of a theatrical production of *Aladdin*. Young or old, receptive or not, everyone was greeted to a hearty welcome the moment you entered his bus. No one was spared his jovial welcome. People loved him; even those who desperately tried to ignore his good nature soon came round.

His contribution revealed itself in his genuine warmth and real acknowledgement of his passengers in a manner parallel to what the Buddhists refer to as 'Loving Kindness'. Beyond his legitimate responsibilities and duty for fare collection and passenger safety his contribution didn't cost anything and impacted on a great number of people in a meaningful way.

Making a contribution is about making a difference where others genuinely benefit from your contribution. This quality of contribution in our lives provides quiet inspiration in the midst of pressurised workloads, constant targets and results-driven work environments. When we share ourselves and our work, without pressure and the need for approval, it increases the quality of rapport we have with others around us and it helps cultivate a deeper sense of connection.

You must give some time to your fellow men. Even if it's a little thing, do something for others — something for which you get no pay but the privilege of doing it.

Albert Schweitzer, theologian and humanitarian

How did it go?

Q. This all sounds well and good if you have the time (and what are the fat chances of that?) and you're not feeling overwhelmed with deadlines at work and a relationship that's about to blow up. I can hardly take care of myself let alone begin to think about my contribution to others. Do you have any suggestions on how to change the way I am feeling?

A. Thanks for your honesty! You're not alone on this one. I suggest keeping this real simple. Let's say you happen to be good at acknowledging others. Throughout the week, without too much push be on the lookout for as many opportunities that arise for you to acknowledge others. If acknowledging is not your thing, choose your personal strength and apply that. Now here's the smart bit. Tap into a variety of ways of giving your acknowledgements. After all, we want to lessen the pressure, not add to it. At the end of the week make an honest observation on how giving acknowledgements makes you feel. You may find that you've made a contribution on a number of occasions without having to work hard at it at all.

Q. What would your advice be to someone like myself who is continually making a difference to those I work with? I actually feel like I should be taking a step back and making less of a contribution. Any words of wisdom?

A. I'm so glad you shared how you feel because you get to give yourself a treat for acknowledging and celebrating the contributions you are already making. Your coaching relationship is as much about celebrating your successes as it is about working through the areas that you wish to improve. When we value our contribution we strengthen our self-esteem and self-worth. Why not draft a list of healthy treats and give yourself a well-earned reward right now? I think you've more than earned it.

44. Making an impact

There's more than meets the eye when it comes to giving a great presentation. If you want to make an impact when presenting, here are some suggestions that should see you coming out on top.

Unless you're Oprah or Larry King you probably have a fair bit of anxiety when it comes to public speaking. But a good presentation can do as much for its audience as it can for the presenter.

A good presentation should inspire and move the presenter as much as it does its audience. We've all sat and listened to or presented (or done both) wooden performances without much heart or soul. There's no one perfect coaching tip that will launch you into becoming a brilliant presenter. But there are many that will support you in becoming better and more wholehearted when you present. The following are a list of presenting tips I have found effective over the years. The tips are given in no particular order. Some will resonate and others won't. Take what you need. The rest will be there for another day. See what catches your eye. Ready? Let's go.

Do thorough research. It's amazing what useful facts and information you'll come across and the momentum you'll create. Audiences love and relate to real-life examples and stories. Be prepared to lose up to 90% of your research information in the final presentation safe in the knowledge that much of your research will

Here's an idea for you...

Log onto the organisation TED, which stands for Technology, Entertainment and Design, and brings together leading thinkers and doers in these sectors in an annual conference for inspiration, sharing ideas and networking. Each presenter has eighteen minutes to present. Prepare an eighteen-minute presentation based on a subject you feel confident and knowledgeable about that you would feel inspired to share or teach others. Think about some of the points raised in this chapter and how this might relate to your presentation. Contact three organisations and offer your presentation for free.

still be with you. Manage any anxieties about the unknown by walking yourself through your presentation. That way you'll be prepared for the unexpected and aware of the things that can and do go wrong.

Surprise your audiences. Do what Canadian coach Andrea Lee calls zigzagging. Just when your audience thinks you will zig, you zag. Watch the video of neuroanatomist (that's brain researcher to you and me) Jill Bolte Taylor at www.ted.com. You'll see her cry, use her whole body, use PowerPoint and hold up a real human brain to her audience (thought I'd put that last point in to see if you're still listening). You might find it hard trying to match showing a human brain, but there's no harm in having a go at something equally surprising. Given her role as a neuroanatomist, showing a human brain was totally relevant to her talk, so make sure your surprise is in context and not just for surprise's sake.

Awkwardness at the start of a talk is OK. I know we're told the opposite but give yourself a break, you're only human. One way of keeping all this in perspective is to think of swans. One year, while leading a retreat in Devon, our peaceful walk was suddenly interrupted by a loud din. It was a herd of swans making the loudest noise ever. They were flying low and there was an unbelievable awkwardness in their flight – but the moment their bodies hit the water, grace opened up; they had found their flow, they had hit their current. Audiences are far more forgiving and compassionate than we give them credit for. Allow yourself a few minutes to find your flow.

Remember why you're there. If you're feeling nervous or anxious, there might be too much focus on you. Get into the present; switch and focus on your audience. What questions do your audience want answering? Find out what they want as part of your research beforehand. Lose the need to impress and think more in terms of inspiring, teaching and sharing.

Find your way of letting the audience know that you have thought about their needs and the content of the presentation. All that extra research may well hold the answer to an audience member's question. Sharing a recent newspaper clipping will show that you've done your homework.

When both are giving [audience and presenter], each then converts what he or she had just received and gives it back. The phenomenon builds on itself. It creates the opposite of a vicious cycle; it creates a delicious cycle.

Fred Gratzon, founder of the Great Midwestern Ice Cream Company

How did it go?

Q. I tend to do lots of preparation and walk myself through the presentation yet on the day I always forget things, lose my focus and end up giving pretty mediocre presentations. I'm feeling under a lot of pressure from the team I work with to pull my socks up. What can I do to get me out of this rut?

A. The first thing to ask is, are you presenting in an area that you feel comfortable with and like? That's often the first sign of a mediocre presentation. Second, what is working well about your presentations? Can you strengthen or build on those areas? Is there another form of presentation that you feel more competent in delivering? I hate PowerPoint so tend to choose other delivery methods. Third, are you the best person to deliver the presentation? Just because it's always been done this way doesn't mean it has to stay the same. Keep observations on your performance. You may be improving each time and just not noticing it.

Q. How can I really engage an audience without losing control of the presentation?

A. I find having a structured plan in front of me (which, ironically, then gives the flexibility to deviate and leave stuff out) does help to keep the session focused and on track while at the same time allowing space for a little deviation or more time for comments. Being clear about the time allocated to interactive exercises also helps.

45. Faking it

Are you waiting until you've got the right qualifications, experiences, references and live on the right street … before you make your next move? Forget it. Instead get ready by 'acting up' and taking on your new role long before it's been officially handed over.

Right now you probably believe you just don't have what it takes. Let's say you lack the confidence to step into a role or career you really have the experience to do.

Perhaps you long to be a manager and the opportunity's come up to do a maternity cover. Instead you find yourself talking yourself out of applying. That's when you apply the techniques of faking it. Don't get me wrong – we're not talking about going to extremes here. No point faking it to be a dentist when you've been trained to be a painter and decorator. But faking it does work when you have either the qualifications or the experience, or both, but just don't believe you'll make the grade.

Faking it is not the same as being an impostor or a fraud. In the television series Making It Big three contestants are up against each other for their dream job. In one episode all three budding wedding planners recognised the name of their mentor as soon as it was mentioned; they knew exactly who he was and the reputation he had within the industry. Contrast this to an episode of America's Next Top Model, where not one of the twelve contestants knew some of the really big names in the industry. The wedding planners may have been stretched into playing on a bigger stage, handling increased pressure and stress and managing budgets quadruple the amount they'd been used to working with but this didn't mean that they didn't have loads of experience and skills that they were also bringing to the table. Faking it pushes you out of comfortable and familiar territory into an uncomfortable one. By suggesting that you fake it, what is really being suggested is that you step up your game.

Researchers at the University of Wake Forest asked a group of 50 students to act like extroverts for 15 minutes in a group even if they didn't feel like it. The more assertive and energetic they were, the happier they felt. The thing is that at some point we've all faked it. It's legitimate whether it be the first day, week or, in some cases, months of a new job (not so much perhaps if you're someone who's paid to save people's lives). But for the better part of the time there's room for not knowing, practising and making mistakes, taking your time to take on responsibility and learning the ropes.

To stretch yourself into faking it, why not try the following?

Go for a position three steps ahead of where you already are. Expose yourself to that environment. Even sending for an application form or updating your CV can find you acting and thinking differently. Take on something bigger than you have ever tackled before. Mel did this: without any prior experience, she founded a festival in her local area that is now a yearly event and a huge success.

If you pretend to be confident for long enough, eventually you will begin not only to feel confident but also to be confident. It worked for many in AA (Alcoholics Anonymous), where the term originated. It was this phrase that encouraged thousands to imagine themselves sober and to stay with the programme that helped them through to sobriety. Don't forget to give yourself a pat on the back. Faking it will mean taking risks and swimming for a while in unfamiliar waters. But you can do it; you know you can.

It requires great daring to dare to be oneself.

Eugene Delacroix, French Romantic artist

How did it go?

Q. I've been offered an opportunity to move into management for the first time. This is something I've always wanted but I'm afraid I'll mess up and lose credibility. Should I wait and get more experience and apply for something later on down the road?

A. I'm assuming you've been offered this post because someone in the organisation is aware of your potential and skill. So going on the assumption that what they feel is correct, take a deep breath and go for it. What do you have to lose? All managing is about learning and it's a steep learning curve. Whatever your experience, you will be able to bring this into future work. Seize the moment now. Act as if you are already the manager you want to be.

Q. I find myself in a strange position. I have the qualifications – and in many cases I am overqualified – for the positions I would really like to work in but don't have the confidence to apply for these posts. Can you help me beat this challenge?

A. One piece of advice: take action now. By the end of the week send off your CV to five companies you want to hire you, including the HR department in the company you are already working for. Remember, confidence comes after the act, not before. Please make this your mantra. When in post your job will be to learn from any mistakes and failings and then to succeed in the areas of your strengths and talents. Rise to the challenge knowing that you do have what it takes.

RESUME

195

46. Building your platforms

How will your expertise, skills and knowledge reach your audience? You'll do that by what we call in coaching 'building your platform'.

Think of your platform as the systems and structures you'll create to communicate and market your business and products.

Two weeks after my first book was published I literally never heard from the marketing manager again. Don't worry, it wasn't personal. It's a very common feature in the publishing world. It was left to me to generate leads and profile my work and attract the attention of the media. I was lucky. I was in the business of running workshops and public speaking. You, on the other hand, may not be in the same position. But that's what's great about building your platform. The tools, systems and structures are available to everyone, no matter what stage you're at in your career or with your product.

I love radio and listen to it as often as I can throughout my day. Radio, especially local radio, is always on the lookout for new stories with unique hooks. That means that right now you stand a very good chance of getting yourself on air.

The first thing I would suggest is getting to know your local stations. What are the styles of the programmes? Which ones cover topics that would be suitable for your input or comment? There's nothing worse than appearing on a radio programme and it becomes obvious that you know nothing about the show. It's your responsibility to do your homework. Not only will you feel better but also you'll come across as more congruent and with integrity.

Don't wait to be invited on a show. If the topic is something you know about, ring up and give your expert opinion. One day, while switching between radio stations, I heard the same person, who specialises in arranging for UK residents to travel to Poland to have dental work done much more cheaply, three times on three different radio stations. Coincidence? No, the front-page news story that day was about the rising cost of dental work in the UK and she didn't wait for them to come to her, she went to them. She waited for her hook and seized her moment. You can bet she got a lot of hits on her site that day. I certainly have made a note to use her services in the future.

By now I hope you are quite excited about the possibilities ahead of you. Here are a few more basic steps you can take to build your platform. Many are easy and accessible.

> **Here's an idea for you...**
>
> Imagine that in the next half an hour the phone will ring from a radio or television programme, asking you to appear live on their show. The media world works fast so they'll probably interview you on the spot about your background, experience and online presence. Draft a four-line script of what you would say in the first twenty seconds that would capture their attention and have them booking you on the spot. You can go on to use this script for future cold calls, media enquiries and first-time introductions.

Write yourself a press release. A friend in marketing saw my press release and offered to rewrite it for me. I know it must have been pretty bad because the one she saw was a version done by moi. Not only did I feel more confident about sending out the new release but I also sent it out more often and I got two radio interviews and a television appearance on the back of her newly amended version.

Set up a blog. They're free and overtaking websites and offer a great way to build your profile on the net. Make sure that whatever you write you share your expertise and knowledge as well as some personal stuff about yourself as you don't want to come across as too stuffy. Focus your material on providing answers to questions for your readers. Take a look at some popular blogs (see, for example, www.sethgodin.com and www.escapefromcubiclenation.com).

Some people think that as soon as you plant a tree, it must bear fruit. We must allow it to grow a bit.

Prince Tunku Putra Abdul Rahman (b. 1903), Malaysian political leader

How did it go?

Q. *I have a very select client group that I want to attract but I have no contacts at all in that industry. Where do I start?*

A. I have to tell you a story about someone I know. She worked full time but was developing a small business baking and elaborately decorating cakes for all occasions. She wanted to break into the celebrity market. So she researched when her favourite music artist was next appearing in the UK and baked him a birthday cake. She made contact with his manager and arranged to deliver the cake backstage at one of his shows. Other commissions have since followed. Be willing to break the rules and to go out on a limb. What's the one thing you could do to break into your niche area? Then do it. If that doesn't work, try another approach.

Q. *I've been sending out my press release on a regular basis and getting no joy. Shall I stop sending it out and focus my efforts elsewhere?*

A. Having been around backstage on radio shows a lot, I've learnt a few things that I'm sure you'll find useful. Staff turnover is really high and it's a pretty stressed environment. So make sure it's going to the right person. Call up and ask for the name of the show's producer and send it in to them. Follow-up etiquette suggests that if you email first time, then it's OK to follow with a phone call. A total of three contacts per pitch is the done thing. Second thing is to get some feedback on your press release from an expert. Sometimes a simple tweak here and there is all that is needed. Third, widen your net and contact radio stations not on your current list.

47. Take time for feedback

How often do you give yourself feedback? Or is it something you shy away from? Feedback can be a really great way to grow quickly and expand your repertoire of skills.

When you really understand the value of feedback you'll end up begging people to bring it on. When communicated in the right manner and spirit, feedback can be a powerful form, enabling you, your business and your career to grow.

When I was growing up, my idea of how to give feedback was really an example of how to give criticism. It wasn't that my parents were deliberately cruel. Not at all. What they lacked were examples from their own lives of how to give quality feedback that wasn't based on a model of focusing entirely on what you did wrong.

Can you recall the last time you either received or offered someone good-quality feedback? If you can, did you ask for the feedback, was it requested or was it just given to you? Giving feedback is a skill, a skill not many of us are taught, which leads to many of us being on the receiving end of clumsy and ill-constructed feedback that causes more damage than it does good. When feedback is done well and thoughtfully it has the potential to inspire and motivate change.

When you work with a coach you have at your disposal someone to offer immediate feedback. Don't forget that feedback is one of the essential elements of good communication. Coaching yourself means you have to work that extra bit harder in ensuring that you create the right environments and relationships for feedback to flourish in, in terms of both feedback that you give and feedback that you receive.

So it makes sense to begin with identifying what exactly goes into the art of giving feedback skilfully. Whilst you will develop the skill of giving feedback over time, this feedback template will support you in the early stages to do this well.

> **Here's an idea for you...**
>
> One way of offering feedback or giving feedback to yourself is to ask and answer these simple questions.
> - What do I think I should do more of? (Be as specific as you can with your examples.) What habits or actions would reap better results or rewards?
> - What could I do less of? (Is there anything that you or someone else could stop doing that would actually improve prospects?)
> - What would I like to stay the same? (Affirm what is being done that already works.)
>
> Try these questions out on yourself first. They're powerful.

- Create the right environment for the feedback to happen by ensuring you're in a positive space and frame of mind. Feedback given from a negative place is bound to offend.
- Base your feedback on the facts and not the person. Focus your feedback towards the main issues and make it clear this is not an analysis of the person.
- Offer feedback as soon as you can after the event. If feedback is given days later you run the risk of reducing the impact and vibrancy of the feedback as

well as ensuring that those of us (moi included) with dodgy memories start to forget some of the facts.

Michelle Collins and Julie K. Richie, founders of Leadership Her Way, have created a feedback model I have found useful.

Three Rs of when to give feedback

- Give it regularly
- Give it right away
- Offer feedback as a remedy to change behaviour with emphasis on reinforcing the specific behaviour you want to continue.

Remember, feedback does not mean there's something wrong with you. Well thought through feedback will stretch and create real opportunities for learning and growth for you, your work and your business. As most people are reluctant to give feedback you'll need to be willing to actively seek it from those who are willing to give it constructively.

Another woman approached me while I was having lunch at the Russian Tea Room in New York and told me that the reason she had become a lawyer was because she had read *Rage of Angels*. To me, that kind of feedback has more meaning than any sales figures. Sidney Sheldon

How did it go?

Q. Recently I gave a close friend some feedback and she took it personally and now refuses to talk to me. Is there anything I can do to make amends?

A. Unfortunately, like most things in life, we can't control other people's reactions. Regardless of how well and sensitively you gave the feedback there may be personal reasons why your friend has responded in this way that are beyond your control. In the meantime, keep the communication lines open by saying sorry about the hurt you may have caused if you haven't done so already. Send a card or a letter, not an email. In cases like this email is considered impersonal and inappropriate. In time, when she's ready, I'm sure she'll come round.

Q. I'm anxious about feedback I have to give a member of my team about her personal appearance. She wears inappropriate outfits that have become the gossip in the office. I feel awkward because she's exceptional in her job. Is there a way I can soften the blow? I know she takes things to heart.

A. Sometimes even those of us giving the feedback may fail to fully appreciate just how valuable our feedback is. So many people have struggled on in life without people offering upfront, directly communicated feedback. How about changing your perspective and imagining that you're handing her a gift in the feedback? Next, decide if she is under-dressing or over-dressing. In your conversation highlight how either approaches can impact her chances for promotion. Start off by validating her strengths and exceptional work. Next, ask her about ways to build her image in the office that would reflect the great work she is doing. You might want to suggest she reads *What You Wear Can Change Your Life* by Trinny Woodall and Susannah Constantine.

48. Who's got your back?

Behind every superhero, idol, famous person, celebrity, genius or everyday person like you and me you'll find a team of people working away behind the scenes to make them who they are. What about building a team of your own?

So what about you? I'm not suggesting you run off and get yourself a PA and start interviewing would-be agents but how about taking a closer look at who's around you and working out who's got your back? Here's what I want you to do.

Grab a blank sheet of paper, or the back of an envelope will do. Pop your name in the middle of the page then, according to closeness or distance, plot your circle of friends on the page. Now do the same but on this page write down the names of all the people who support and take care of you in other ways. This might include people like your hairdresser, the cleaner, your accountant, your doctor and your web designer. Your Dream Team makes it possible for you to do what you do well. Each one makes an important contribution both to your well-being and your productivity and efficiency. Quite often it's easy to ignore the value that these individuals bring to the quality of our lives.

Now let's take a review of both your friendships and your Dream Team. Go through each name one by one and on a scale of 1–10, with 10 meaning the relationship is going really great and 1 meaning it's not so great, review each of your relationships. You can do this by asking yourself questions like: Who motivates and rocks me? Who sinks or drains my energy? Is there anyone on the list who honestly drains my energy and makes me sick? Is the balance right in my friendships? Is there a good flow between giving and receiving? Are my roles fluid and flexible? Your answers may point to a friendship that has fizzled out or the need to change or let go of a member of your team. Perhaps the review will throw light on a resentment that hasn't been cleared up or the need to make a special effort to let someone know how much you care or how much their service is appreciated. Now's the time to take action.

I decided to build a team around me based on my weaknesses, things I didn't have time to do or was hopeless at doing. So whilst I can do my taxes (I flunked maths at school) I employ an accountant who is much more passionate and competent about figures. No problem or challenge around my taxes is too big or too small for Sam. In the same way my graphic designer is a godsend. Having her on my team

> **Here's an idea for you...**
>
> Arrange for a group of friends to support you in resolving a personal challenge. An hour will do fine. Arranging food or drinks always makes the invitation a bit more inviting. But stick to your agenda first, then socialise. Arrange to meet in a quiet space where you won't be distracted. In the first ten minutes outline your challenge or issue. The group then has 30 minutes to ask you a series of questions or make comments. Listen and take note of the questions and the comments. At the end take another ten minutes to share your thoughts and reflections on what's been said, thank your guests and close the proceedings. This is a variation on the Quaker practice called the Clearness Committee.

means the difference between merely having a creative idea and taking my idea and turning it into a workable and attractive tool within 48 hours. Your Dream Team needs to include individuals better qualified to support you and your business.

Don't forget to include individuals who take care of your body, your soul, your finances, your car, your teeth, your feet, your holidays, your hair and your home. It's so important to develop good rapport with each one. At the end of the day you want everyone on your side from the handyman to the mortgage adviser. Invest in your relationships with everyone on your team and you can't go wrong.

I've been blessed with friends who do things rather than buy things. Maeve Binchy, Irish writer

How did it go?

Q. I've just moved to London and I am finding it hard to make new friends. I'm saving for a deposit to buy a flat so can't get home often. How can I make new friends?

A. London is overflowing with numerous opportunities to make new friends. The first obvious place is within your professional area of work. Join a professional networking group. There'll be plenty of network groups in your area. Love books? Then how about joining the local library reading group? Next think about your passions. Is it dance, or is it gardening? There'll be a local group somewhere. The more people you get to talk to over time, the more connections you will make. I would say give it time and don't give up; sooner or later you will strike gold.

Q. My business partner ripped me off and now I am really wary of trusting people, which has resulted in me taking on too much. What can I do to let go and learn to trust again?

A. First, I am sorry to hear about what happened. Being done over is never nice, especially when it's been done by someone we trust. In order to move on it's important that you gain perspective on the situation. You will learn to trust others again, perhaps in a different way. But it will take time. It's really important for you to gather together what you learnt from the situation and to use your experience and intuition in future relationships. Start by delegating small tasks more and allowing room for mistakes. The thing about trust is once it's been broken the way to getting it back is to risk and trust again.

Be your own best life coach

49. Reaching out

When it comes to networking, don't sweat the small stuff.

Does networking feel like a chore? By keeping it simple and following some easy networking etiquette, with very little effort you'll be on your way to making meaningful connections.

We've become a world of amateur and professional networkers. Networking is the new marketing. Whilst a few of us are gifted networkers, the rest of us are content to just get by with handing out business cards and talking to as many people as we can. Handing out ten business cards at an event is not a triumph if you're never going to follow up those contacts again. Better to make one contact and make it well than nine others that go nowhere. Small details can make a big difference when networking.

There's etiquette to receiving a business card that will imprint you in the person's memory and them in yours. The best way to receive a business card is to give one. Once the card is handed over don't just take the card and place it in your wallet; take a few seconds to glance over the details. Comment on anything that stands out about the card. People frequently tell me how much they love the design of my business card. It's a great opener to my story about designing that card in ten minutes. Follow this up by writing down any details about the person, where you met or reasons for getting in contact on the card itself. This is a really warm way of showing your genuine interest in having met. Make people feel important in order to make yourself important to them.

Remember the small stuff and details about people you talk with. Small touches can make a memorable imprint. Make sure you're practising active listening. It's surprising how many people zone out and aren't even aware of doing it. Details like remembering someone's name, offering to get them a drink, offering them a contact or recommendation early in your conversation go down well and leave a lasting impression.

Make an effort to remember and repeat specific details you hear in conversations. See if you can make connections. I'm sure you've experienced a moment in a conversation where you say, 'Oh, I just spoke with someone who knows all about that. Would you like to be introduced?' Not only have you remembered what someone else has said, but you've also helped solve someone else's problem, and you've flagged yourself up as a useful contact.

Be open to networking anywhere, be it at the school gates, the waiting room of the doctor's surgery or dinner at a friend's house. A friend met the head of a consultancy on a train ride from Nottingham to London. They got talking and it turns out that she'd worked in the area in which the consultant was just about to pitch for a major contract. Naturally she happily shared her knowledge and expertise and by the end of the journey had been offered work with the consultancy, which she accepted. I landed a major speaking engagement in New York at a social engagement in Washington DC where I knew only one other person. Everywhere's a potential networking opportunity.

Lower your expectations when networking. This might seem strange coming from me. But here's why. When you lower your expectations you take the pressure off yourself, which improves your chances of coming across relaxed, open and approachable. Don't expect to create rapport with everyone. It's unrealistic and a huge time waster.

To really get the most out of networking think not what you can get but what you can give. I know it's the other way round from what most of us have been taught and for many of us it will require a change in mindset. I have certainly found this the best way to network; sharing information and connecting people to resources and to each other offers a stress-free way to make real and meaningful contact with others. It's a genuine way of gaining credibility and business trust, which at the end of the day is what networking is all about.

There's an 80% better chance that your next position will come from someone you know.

Robert Holden, author and founder of The Happiness Project

How did it go?

Q. I really find it hard to start off conversations, particularly at formal networking events. Any suggestions?

A. Develop easy questions beforehand that hook people into the conversation. These don't have to be grand or complicated. Simple does it: 'Hi, what did you think of the speaker?' 'Is the red wine any good?' 'Do you know any good places to go around here for a bite to eat?' 'How do you know the host?' One good question may be enough to get your conversation going.

Q. I've a really poor memory and really do find it hard to remember names and even the content of conversations I have with people. Is there any hope for someone like me?

A. I have a question to ask you. Do you prefer writing emails to speaking to people? I have a hunch that you'd prefer email. If the answer is yes then focusing on virtual networking is the best way forward for someone like yourself. One thing that will keep you in the loop is to make sure you get contact details from everyone you meet and you send them a follow-up email within 24 hours of meeting them. It will not only help them to keep you fresh in their memory but will also help solidify your memory of them in yours.

50. Money is your friend

Ever done a financial detox? No it doesn't mean emptying your bank account and giving all your money away. Instead, let's face some home truths and clean up our financial act.

There's a reason why we say keep an eye on the money. That's because people who have money, enjoy money and are successful with money keep close track of their money and how they spend it. So how about a little bit of financial detoxification?

It's always a good idea to start at the root of a problem because if we don't get to the root cause we're only touching the surface of the problem. Many of your challenges with money will have been embedded in what you learnt about money when you were a child. Let's start by recalling the first time you remember having a negative experience around money.

Describe the experience in a few sentences in your notebook then sit back and take a few deep breaths. Now ask yourself, what did I take that experience to mean to me? Take another deep breath. Continue by answering the following questions. What or how does that meaning play out in my relationship to money right now? Take another deep breath. How is this behaviour serving me? Is it

Here's an idea for you...

Be an agent of change and delight for the next week. Think of ways in which you can practise random acts of kindness. Let someone go in front of you in a queue. Give up your seat on a packed train to someone who looks more tired and worn out than you. Deliver a home-cooked meal to a friend who's feeling a bit down.
Or maybe you'll want to do something like the strangers who sat next to me and two friends at dinner (to whom we did speak briefly) who anonymously paid for our meal. We only found out when the waiters told us long after they had left.

working positively for me or is it costing me? If it's not working for me, what is the real cost to me – lack of self-esteem, guilt, lack of energy? Take a deep breath. Finish off by quickly answering this question: If I knew what changes to make to the way I handle my finances these would be (complete the sentence).

Phew, what did you discover? Did you notice that you either mirrored or rebelled against your parents' attitude to money? Did you feel a need to forgive yourself for anything? You may start to make lots of connections; write down your observations in your notebook. They'll come in handy for the next exercise.

At this point it's a good idea to take a break. You may be finding this work around money very emotional. Money is both an emotional and an energetic force so don't be shocked by how you might be feeling. This might be a good point to give yourself a comfort treat before you continue.

Detoxing is letting go of waste and toxins that are harmful to our system. Make a list of incomplete or unresolved financial issues from your past. This could be an unpaid debt or a poor financial decision. For years I felt guilty and ashamed about neglecting to pay a friend for some beautiful furniture I'd bought from her. Every time visitors commented on the beauty of the furniture I could never really enjoy their appreciation of the items because of the unresolved payment. Finally I summoned up the courage to pay her what I believed I owed her. It felt like a great weight had been lifted. When I did a similar list this item was really high on the agenda. Once you have listed your issues number them. Take your top three issues and outline three steps that will mean taking action to resolve the issue. Now get to work. It may take some weeks or even months to see results. Be patient. You may be undoing years of work.

As you work your way through your list you may begin to uncover the reason why you misused money, overspent or disrespected friendships or family members because of money. For a while your financial detox may feel like it's making things worse rather than better. This is only a short-term experience. The work you are doing now will have far-reaching long-term implications. So keep going. You're worth every penny of your time and investment.

And if you want to make amends right now, follow the example of Oprah Winfrey who recently gave each member of her audience a sum of money to do good in their communities. A management company in the US has since followed suit, giving its employees money to give away to someone else in need. Start today; give something away.

True financial freedom lies in defining ourselves, by who and what we are, not by what we do or don't have. Suze Orman, financial adviser

How did it go?

Q. I've tried contacting someone I owe money to and I can't get in touch with them. What should I do?

A. Two things: take double the amount of money that is owed. Put half the amount in a savings account and leave it there for one year. That feels like a reasonable amount of time to see if they get in contact. Take the second half of the money and donate it to charity. This should help shake off any guilt that only renders you powerless and helpless (which are not powerful places to make financial decisions from).

Q. I owe similar amounts to both individuals and companies. Who should I pay off first?

A. It's custom to honour payments to individuals first, especially if they fall into the category of friends or family members. But I would suggest contacting your creditors and setting up a minimum repayment while you concentrate on paying off the personal debts. Either way, communicate with all your creditors.

51. How to get rich on a not so rich salary

True wealth, both in terms of personal and financial wealth, comes from valuing who you are rather than how much you have deposited in the bank. All the money in the world won't buy you happiness.

Do you remember all those lottery winners who won millions and then lost it all? All the money in the world didn't make them rich. What if you could work out what you were worth that wasn't based on your financial net worth but was based on your Life net worth?

I first came across this exercise years ago in a book called *Money Magic*, written by Deborah L. Price. At the time I was in quite a lot of debt and wasn't making as much money as I would have liked to. I devoured the whole book in two days. As with everything, I skipped some exercises but others moved me to the page. The Life Bank exercise made sense. This is how it works. If it worked for me and for many of my clients, I am sure it will work for you. In your notebook answer the following questions:

How old are you?

How many life hours have you spent? That's your age (I'm 46) times 365 (days in the year) times 24 (hours in the day). For example, I have spent 402,960 life hours. It certainly puts a different perspective on things when you look at your life in the context of the number of hours you've lived.

How have you spent your time?

Your answer to this question can include a list of all the things you've done in your lifetime that make you feel good about who you are and the things you have done that have been meaningful to you. This is not about the things you have. Next, make a list of all the things you would still like to do that would continue to give you great fulfilment and satisfaction.

Finally, how many days are you currently spending towards meeting these personal goals?

I found that it took me a few days to gather together all the things I wanted to include in my inventory. Once you feel you have a near enough complete list, spend several minutes really taking in what you've written. How do you feel about your list? How does it feel when you look at the number of hours of your life that you've already spent? Does it make you more discerning now about how you will spend your time and money in the future? Are you really getting to live the life you want or is the way you're spending your time actually robbing you of this?

This exercise stretches you to consider and appreciate your worth beyond the trappings of your financial identity. I have seen individuals on the brink of bankruptcy feel hope after completing this exercise and in many cases individuals have turned their lives around.

Your goal is to coach yourself to value the time that's been spent and the time you have left to consciously decide how you will spend it.

Whatever you have gone through, you still have your whole life ahead of you. It's a joy when individuals in my coaching practice from all different income levels really get this. When they really get that what really matters is how they see themselves beyond what they earn. Hold on to the thought that your self-worth cannot be measured by your net worth. This recognition in and of itself often marks a huge turning point where money flows even more in their lives.

There's a great difference between earning a great deal of money and being rich.

Marlene Dietrich, actress

How did it go?

Q. I've been left a considerable amount of money by a relative. But instead of enjoying myself I have found myself worrying and not touching the money at all. How can I enjoy my gift as well as take care of the money that's been left?

A. Lucky you. Go through the Life Bank exercise and choose one item from the list of personal goals and take the funds and pay for it. No deliberating and no 'I can't afford it' thoughts. Just do it, that's an order. Each year choose something from the list and, if the money allows it, use the gift to fund it. What about gifting 10% or more of what you've been left to a charity that you'd love to support? That feeling of contributing to a worthwhile cause will leave you feeling really good.

Q. I live on a student loan and small grant plus handouts from my family. My parents still have a lot of financial responsibilities and I hate to rely on them for funds. It's so important that I budget but also that I have a good time. How much would you suggest I budget and enjoy myself?

A. My daughter is in her second year at university so I know how important it is to get that balance. You won't need to spend loads of money to feel good. Have some fun coming up with a list of activities you could enjoy doing for free or that cost very little at all. There's probably so much you could do and get involved in where you live now that would give you a rich experience. Start off with the website for your local authority. Find out what activities and memberships are on offer from your student union. Talk to people from the area and find out great things to do locally that cost next to nothing.

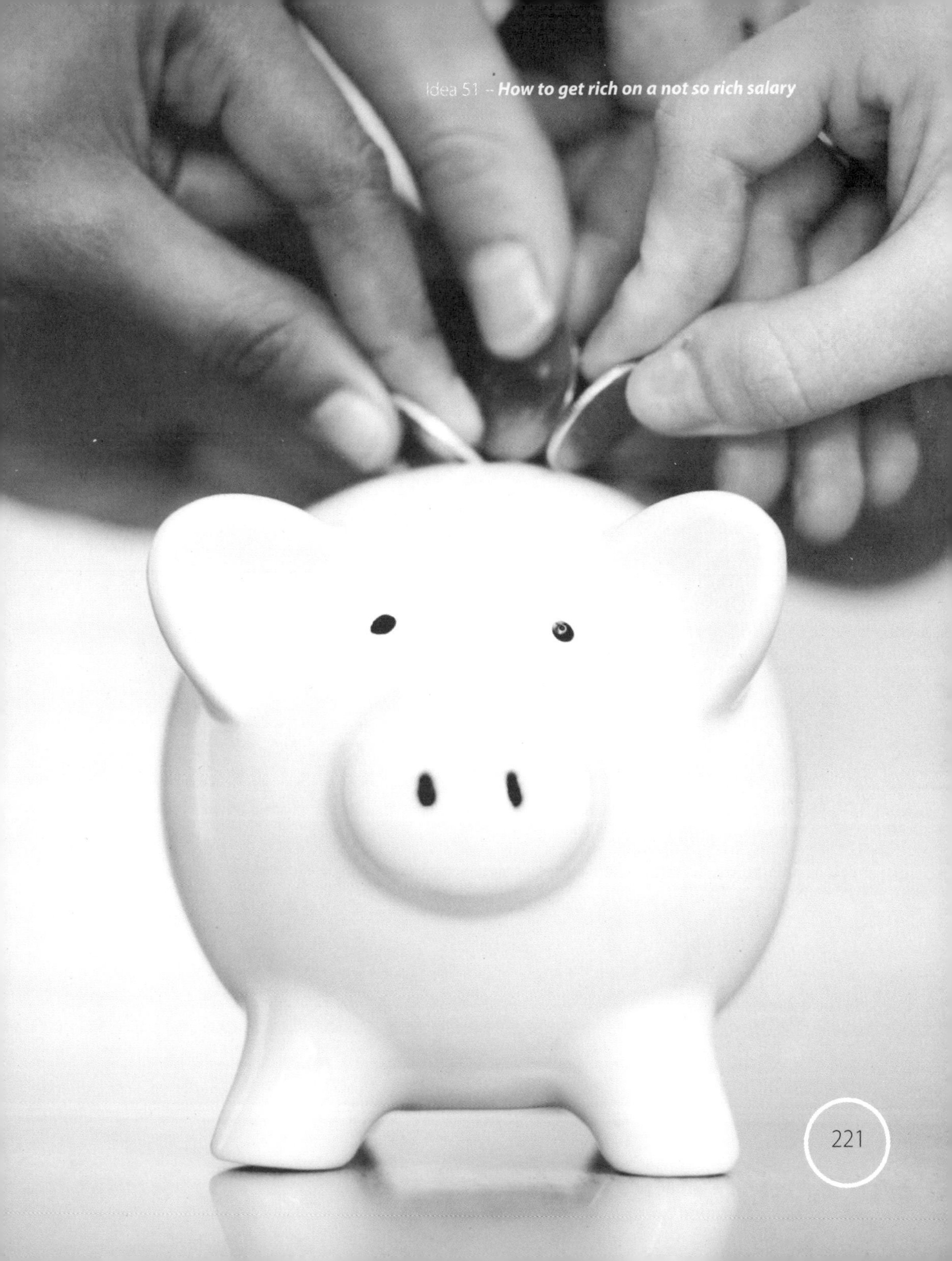

52. Future perfect

Next stop, your future life. Have serious fun creating a compelling vision for your future that's creative and inspiring. Your future lies in your hands.

A really good starting point is to begin with the end in mind. Think about where you want to be and begin to work your way backwards.

I hope that right now you're feeling empowered and inspired to take charge of your one beautiful life. By now you should be in a flow and feeling confident about making time to hang out with yourself. It's now time to design your future. Here's what I want you to do. This is as much an adventure in your creativity as it is in introducing more play and fun into your life.

Go to an art or stationery shop and purchase a large sheet of poster paper, probably covering at least the size of eight A4 sheets and some glue. Gather together a range of magazines from health and lifestyle women's magazines and home and garden magazines to computer and men's lifestyle magazines. It's important if you're buying your magazines off the shelf to have a flick through the magazines first to make sure you like the kinds of images they carry. Set aside an hour or more. Clear a space in a room and get everything out. Make sure you're wearing comfortable clothing so you can move around easily. You're going to make a collage of your future. Start off by leafing through the magazines and tearing out images, words and ideas that move you and inspire you. You don't have to worry about why you've been inspired but it might get you thinking about what areas of your life you would like that image to reflect. As you relax into the exercise you'll build up momentum. When you're doing your collage you'll probably experience what psychologists call the flow, being totally involved in an activity and totally focused on what you are doing in the present moment. Once you have a pile of images, start putting together your collage, using the images to reflect how you would like your life to be in the future.

Think big, think outside the box and push your own expectations about what is really possible for you. I love making collages. I get lost in the activity and it always leaves me feeling uplifted, energised and inspired. Over the years I have made several collages, marking different stages of my life, and it's quite amazing how much of the stuff that I depicted in them has come true. I think creating a collage is a really magical experience.

The next step is often overlooked and yet it is an important one. What you do with your collage does make a difference. I had a friend who turned one half of a wall in her living room, from ceiling to floor, into a huge vision map. It was

> **Here's an idea for you...**
>
> Solution-Focused Coaching came up with the idea of the miracle question. The miracle question bypasses your problems and challenges and invites you to project yourself forward into what they describe as the 'Future Perfect'. Ask yourself the miracle questions.
>
> "Suppose a miracle happened tonight: what would be different about your life?" Get specific by digging further. What will you be doing? What will you be saying? What will other people notice that's different about you? Keep probing what your miracle will look and feel like. Get as specific as you can. See whether there is more by asking, 'What else?'

breathtaking to look at. Think about where you'll display your collage, preferably where you can see it every day. Now the work begins of programming these images into your mind so that they become a part of you. Imagine yourself in front of your vision map. Choose one particular image or scene from your vision map. Close your eyes and imagine yourself feeling, seeing, tasting, sensing and hearing everything associated with that particular scene. When you have made your connections, imagine yourself walking backwards from the scene from your vision map into this present moment. Ask yourself what new steps and actions you will need to take to move this area of your life on to a whole new level.

I looked always outside of myself to see what I could make the world give me, instead of looking within myself to see what was there.

Belle Livingstone, adventurer and writer

How did it go?

Q. I did the collage, as suggested, which I really enjoyed and then when I did the miracle question I ended up with two different visions. Which one should I go with?

A. Which one do you feel most drawn to? Your vision may not unfold in exactly the way you have illustrated it on your collage or expressed in your responses to your miracle questions. But from what you've shared it sounds like there are lots of options available to you and that is what is being reflected back. I would just get started on one action and see what happens. I don't think it will be long before you know what path to follow.

Q. My family loved the vision collage I made on a course at work. Now they all want to do one. Is it best to do one as a family or should we all do our own?

A. It's great that your family loves the idea of vision maps. What about doing both? This could be a great activity for your family to plan and get engaged in. Why not make a whole event out of it? Get to work collecting magazines from schoolmates and colleagues. Set yourself a budget (say, £20) and purchase magazines, paper and a glue sick (very important). When the collages are complete, create a simple ritual. You could invite each member to talk about what the collage means to them. Have everyone write something to accompany the collage. Have the family decide where in the home the collage will be displayed.

Acknowledgements

No writer writes a book entirely on their own and I'm no exception. There are many people past and present who are responsible for helping me birth the book you now have in your hands. First off I would like to say a big thank you to the coaches and supervisors who have generously worked with me over the last ten years. Not only has each one touched me in very profound ways but each has been responsible for birthing my own inner coach. In no particular order I would like to thank: Carolyn Free-Pearce, Susan Ingram, Sue Lee, Lynda Field, Eric Maisel, Henri Seebohm, Lili Levy, Robert Holden, Dr Simon Western, Laura Berman Fortgang and Mark Forster.

There have been a few people who sometimes without even knowing it have been a rock of inspiration and I appreciate their belief in my work and my writing. I would especially like to say a big thank you to the following fellow writers and friends: Suzette Clough, Nick Williams, Julia McCuthchen, Steve Nobel, Judy Reeves, Akima Thomas and Michelle Springer-Benjamin.

Three people in particular were constant in giving feedback on the text throughout the period of writing this book. They never faltered in making the time and offering their insights and critiques. What can I say but a big hug and thank you to my readers: Delroy Constantine-Simms, Marcia Gayle and Sandy Parris. And a big thanks to Gita Patel who brought the vision of my Wheel of Life Tree to life in a great design – I loved working with you, Gita.

A very special thank you to Elizabeth Lesser and the staff from the Omega retreat centre in New York who graciously gifted me with a two-week stay at Omega where this book came to life. My stay there in the summer of last year marked a turning point for me.

My own life has been continually inspired and supported by the wonderful Sharron Wallace and my daughter Aida. Thank you both for being true family to me.

In particular I owe my family big time. They, in their own ways, have been teaching me for years, things I am only now coming to realise were and are intended as gifts. I may not have been the greatest student but I hope I am becoming a much more gracious and grateful learner.

I cannot end without saying thank you to the wonderful people I have coached over the last few years, people who have attended my workshops and the original members of the Moon wRites writing group. Special thanks for being patient go out to my editors Rebecca and Katherine from Infinite Ideas. And an extra special shout goes out to all the women and staff at Clean Break Theatre Company, in particular Tracey, Jacquie, Anna, Ella and Sam.

And finally I dedicate this book to my dad Carlisle Sylvian Holder whose recent passing has left a big hole in my life but whose face would have lit up with a smile knowing that this book is now complete.

A big hug to your own inner coach. I know you can, and will, do it.

Jackee

Be your own best life coach

The Big Read: 52 books to read in a year

Every year I devour a huge quantity of self-help and personal development books. But among the many only a few leave a lasting mark. These are books I can return to year after year and still be excited by what I read and still find the text refreshing. Some have become daily companions, often by my side. I hope that you will find one or two from the list that will have the same impact for you. The list contains 52 recommendations, so hopefully you'll keep yourself busy throughout the year.

Coaching

Live Your Best Life; Now What? 90 Days To A New Life Direction; and *Take Yourself To The Top*, by Laura Berman Fortgang (www.laurabermanfortgang.com)

Take Time For Your Life; and *Life Makeovers*, by Cheryl Richardson (www.cherylrichardson.com)

The Ten-Minute Life Coach, by Fiona Harrold (www.fionaharrold.com)

Transform Your Life, by Penny Ferguson (www.pennyferguson.com)

Becoming A Professional Life Coach, by Patrick Williams and Diane S. Menendez (www.lifecoachtraining.com)

The Big Book of Me, by Nina Grunfeld (www.lifeclubs.co.uk)

Time management

Seven Habits Of Highly Effective People, by Steven Covey (www.stevencovey.com)

Do It Tomorrow; and *Get Everything Done And Still Have Time To Play*, by Mark Forster (www.markforster.net)

Goals and creative dreams

Make Your Creative Dreams Real, by Sark (www.planetsark.com)
How To Make Your Dreams Come True, by Mark Forster
 (www.markforster.net)
The Right Questions, by Debbie Ford (www.debbieford.com)
The Artist's Way; and *The Sound Of Paper*, by Julia Cameron (www.theartistsway.com)
Creative Licence, by Danny Gregory (www.dannygregory.com)
The Creativity Book, by Eric Maisel (www.ericmaisel.com)
You Can Have What You Want, by Michael Neill (www.geniuscatalyst.com)

Life purpose

I Will Not Die An Unlived Life, by Dawna Markova (www.dawnamarkova.com)
Callings, by Gregg Levoy (www.gregglevoy.com)
The Work We Were Born To Do, by Nick Williams (www.Nick-Williams.com)
Crossing The Unknown Sea, by David Whyte (www.davidwhyte.com)
Everything I've Ever Learned About Change, by Lesley Garner (www.lesleygarner.com)
What Should I Do With My Life? by Po Bronson (www.pobronson.com)
Finding Your Own North Star and *Steering By Starlight*, by Martha Beck
 (www.marthabeck.com)
MePLC – Your Life Is Your Business, by Pascoe Sawyers (www.meplc.co.uk)
Go Put Your Strengths To Work, by Marcus Buckingham
 (www.marcusbuckingham.com)
Money, A Memoir, by Liz Perle (www.moneyamemoir.com)
Transitions, by William Bridges (www.wmbridges.com)
The Art of Possibility, by Rosamund Stone Zander and Benjamin Zander
 (www.benjaminzander.com, www.rosamundzander.com)
Between Trapezes, by Gail Blanke (www.betweentrapezes.com)

Communication and business

Fierce Conversations, by Susan Scott (www.fierceinc.com)

Difficult Conversations, by Douglas Stone, Bruce Patton and Sheila Heen
(www.difficultconversations.com)

Time To Think, by Nancy Kline (www.timetothink.com/uk)

The Feeling Good Handbook, by David D. Burns (www.feelinggood.com)

They F*** You Up, by Oliver James (www.selfishcapitalist.com)

Emotional Alchemy, by Tara Bennett Goleman
(www.emotionalalchemy.com)

The E-Myth Revisited, by Michael E. Gerber (www.e-myth.com)

The Tipping Point, by Malcolm Gladwell (www.gladwell.com)

Success Principles, by Jack Canfield (www.jackcanfield.com)

Success Intelligence, by Robert Holden (www.happiness.co.uk)

Self care

Soul Purpose, by Jackee Holder (www.jackeeholder.com)

The Joy Of Burnout, by Dr Dina Glouberman (www.imagework.co.uk)

Simple Abundance; Something More; and *Romancing The Ordinary*, by Sarah
Ban Breathnach (www.simpleabundance.com)

The Woman's Retreat Book, by Jennifer Louden (www.comfortqueen.com;
and www.jenniferlouden.com)

Twenty-Minute Retreats, by Dr Rachel Harris (www.soulfulliving.com)

Pure Bliss, by Gill Edwards (www.livingmagically.com)

Spiritual Divorce, by Debbie Ford (www.debbieford.com)

The end...

Or is it a new beginning?

We hope that these ideas will have helped give you a new zest for life. Perhaps you were looking for ideas to help you work out your goals in life, wanted to find out how to make your relationship work or were wondering what to do next in your career. Maybe you'd even hit rock bottom. Whatever your circumstances were we hope that these ideas have helped you get your life back on track.

So why not let us know about it? Tell us how you got on. What did it for you – which ideas really helped you think clearly about your life? Maybe you've got some tips of your own that you'd like to share. And if you liked this book you may find we have even more brilliant ideas that could help change other areas of your life for the better.

You'll find the Infinite Ideas crew waiting for you online at www.infideas.com.

Or if you prefer to write, then send your letters to:
Be your own best life coach
Infinite Ideas Ltd
36 St Giles, Oxford, OX1 3LD, United Kingdom

We want to know what you think, because we're all working on making our lives better too. Give us your feedback and you could win a copy of another **52 Brilliant Ideas** book of your choice. Or maybe get a crack at writing your own.

Good luck. Be brilliant.

Offer one

Cash in your ideas

We hope you enjoy this book. We hope it inspires, amuses, educates and entertains you. But we don't assume that you're a novice, or that this is the first book that you've bought on the subject. You've got ideas of your own. Maybe our author has missed an idea that you use successfully. If so, why not send it to yourauthormissedatrick@infideas.com, and if we like it we'll post it on our bulletin board. Better still, if your idea makes it into print we'll send you four books of your choice or the cash equivalent. You'll be fully credited so that everyone knows you've had another Brilliant Idea.

Offer two

How could you refuse?

Amazing discounts on bulk quantities of Infinite Ideas books are available to corporations, professional associations and other organisations.

For details call us on:
+44 (0)1865 514888
Fax: +44 (0)1865 514777
or email: info@infideas.com

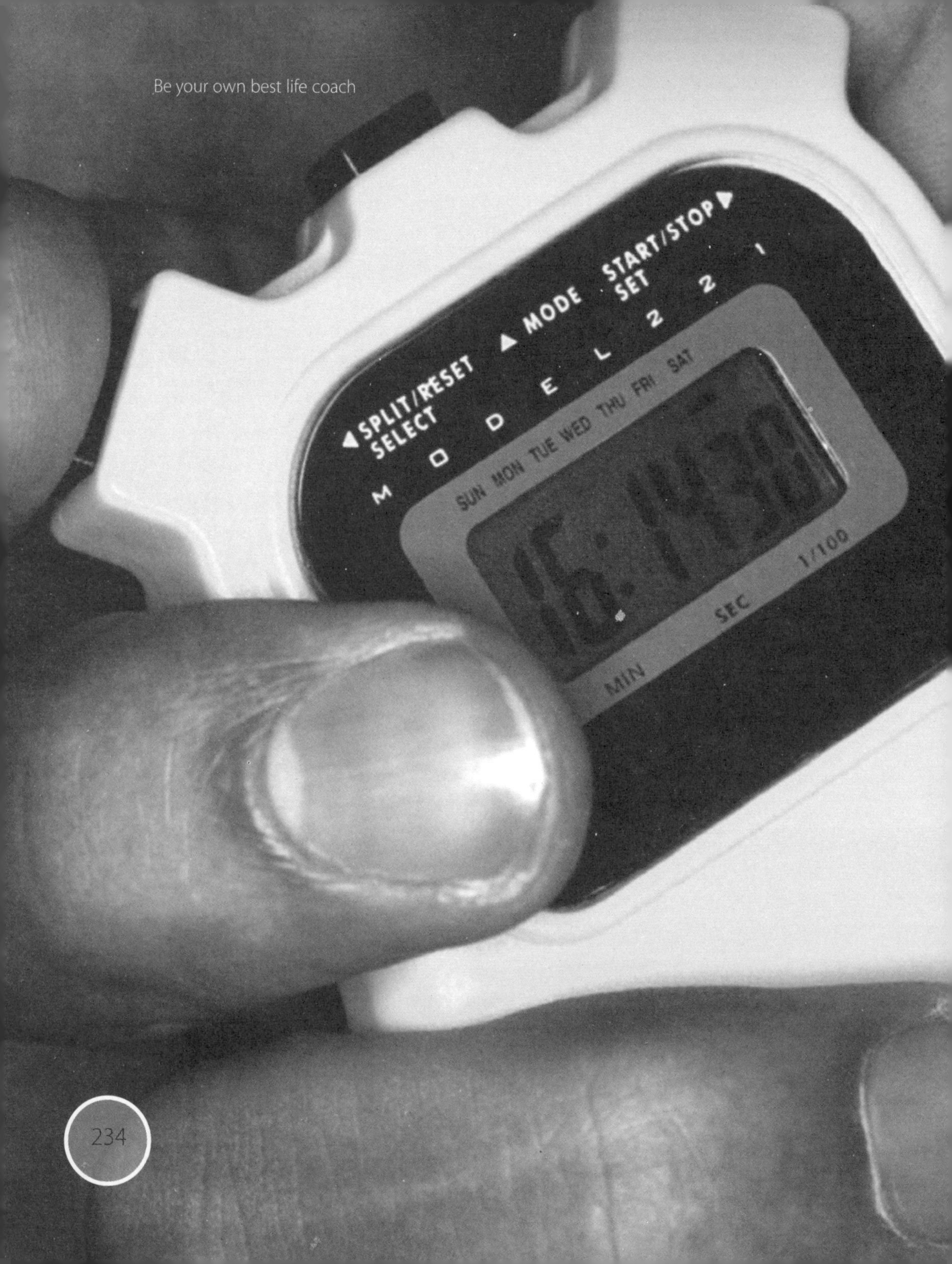
SPLIT/RESET
SELECT
MODE
START/STOP
SET
M O D E L 2 2 1
SUN MON TUE WED THU FRI SAT
MIN
SEC
1/100

Where it's at...